VANITY

GLUTTONY

ENVY

DISHONOR

THE SECRETS TO GENERATIONAL CURSES

POVERTY

RACISM

REBELLION

ALEXANDER PAGANI

VANITY

GLUTTONY

ENVY

DISHONOR

THE
SECRETS TO
GENERATIONAL
CURSES

POVERTY

RACISM

REBELLION

CHARISMA HOUSE

While the author has made every effort to provide accurate internet addresses at the time of publication, neither the publisher nor the author assumes any responsibility for errors or for changes that occur after publication. Further, the publisher does not have any control over and does not assume any responsibility for author or third-party websites or their content.

For more Spirit-led resources, visit charismahouse.com and the author's website at alexanderpagani.com.

Cataloging-in-Publication Data is on file with the Library of Congress.
International Standard Book Number: 978-1-62999-605-9
E-book ISBN: 978-1-62999-606-6

2 2023
Printed in the United States of America

Most Charisma Media products are available at special quantity discounts for bulk purchase for sales promotions, premiums, fund-raising, and educational needs. For details, call us at (407) 333-0600 or visit our website at www.charismamedia.com.

CONTENTS

ACKNOWLEDGMENTS

To the Holy Spirit, thank You for granting me wisdom and insight into the mysteries of the kingdom and entrusting me with the secrets to generational curses to continue Your work of setting the captive free.

To my Lord and Savior, Jesus Christ, thank You for choosing and entrusting me with this ministry.

To my heavenly Father, I'm eternally grateful to You for giving my life purpose and meaning. You're worthy to receive all glory, honor, majesty, and power!

To my loving wife and best friend, Ibelize Pagani (aka Momma Pagani), thank you for believing in me and understanding God's call on my life by sharing me with the world. I love you!

To my apostolic covering, Jabula New Life Ministries International, and its founder, Bishop Tudor Bismark; current presbytery; and presiding bishops, Bishop Hugh Daniel Smith and Bishop Rodrick Roberts, words can't express my gratitude. You took me in when I was a ministerial vagabond and formed me into the man of God I am today. Thank you!

To all the churches and fivefold leaders under my covering through Amazing Church Global—Apostle Jason and Sonia Welsh, Apostles Daniel and Natrietia McClendon, Apostles Armando and Latisha Muniz, Apostles

Stevan and Jacqueline Chinkhan, Apostles Felani and Lele Poe, Prophets Kimani and Datnee Smith, and Apostles Ricardo and Vanessa Alvarez—our movement will be marked with the same blessings of the tribe of Asher! We will eat the delicacies of kings and bathe our feet in new wine! I love you.

To my fellow demon slayers, Isaiah Saldivar, Mike Signorelli, and Vlad Savchuck, in such a short time God put us together, and we're impacting the world together. Our friendship will leave a mark on this digital era that can't be erased as we carry this gospel of Jesus Christ all through social media! We are the digital gatekeepers of this generation, and together we will steer it closer to Christ. Love you.

To pastor Greg Locke, words can't convey my heartfelt thanks for what you've done for our first book, *The Secrets to Deliverance*, by highlighting it in your movie *Come Out in Jesus Name*. Only when we stand before God will we know the impact you've made through your obedience in allowing me to be part of your movie. I love you, and thank you, my friend!

To my best friends, Pastors Emmanuel and Gretchen Gonzalez, you've been with me from beginning and believed in me when no one heard my voice in the back side of the Bronx in the early days of social media. Now the whole world is listening. In the times I wanted to just quit on deliverance because I felt no one cared and that it wasn't worth spending so much time and energy on revelation nobody wanted to embrace, you encouraged me to keep pioneering because in due time there would be a breakthrough. Well, you're seeing the fruit of your behind-the-scenes effort, and that's why wherever I go, I'm taking you with me! I love you!

CHAPTER 1

STUMBLING AND SEARCHING: THE MYSTERY OF THE CURSE

These two women serve as an *illustration* of God's two covenants. The first woman, Hagar, represents Mount Sinai where people received the law that enslaved them. And now Jerusalem is just like Mount Sinai in Arabia, because she and her children live in slavery to the law. But the other woman, Sarah, represents the heavenly Jerusalem. She is the free woman, and she is our mother.

—GALATIANS 4:24–26

Who serve unto the example and *shadow* of heavenly things, as Moses was admonished of God when he was about to make the tabernacle: for, See, saith he, that thou make all things according to the pattern showed to thee in the mount.

—HEBREWS 8:5, KJV

Now Adam is a *figure*, a representation of Christ, who was yet to come.

—ROMANS 5:14

For the *mystery* of iniquity doth already work: only he who now letteth will let, until he be taken out of the way.

—2 THESSALONIANS 2:7, KJV

THE REVELATION OF generational curses is not easily defined or outlined in Scripture the way many other things are. Generational curses can only be discovered two ways: 1) by *stumbling* upon them unintentionally or 2) by *searching* for them intentionally. The first way reminds me of the parable Jesus told about a person who stumbles across something hidden in a field (Matt. 13:44), only in this instance we "trip" over the mystifying phenomenon known as generational curses. This "stumbling" usually happens when a believer is talking with another believer, and the Holy Spirit brings to light previously unnoticed hereditary patterns of behavior and identifies them as the root cause of their struggle. The person realizes they've stumbled upon a great revelation and does whatever they can to obtain further understanding on the topic.

The second way of discovery happens when someone has been made fully aware of this treasure—either by divine direction or through another means—and intentionally searches for it. Once again, we find a parable of Jesus (Matt. 13:45) that illustrates how we can go in search of truth until we discover it. It is my belief that most great truths are discovered these two ways: stumbling and searching. The late Myles Munroe summed it up when he gave his assessment of the underlying theme to the parables of Jesus: "Nothing is yours until you discover it."

To further drive this point, the Book of Proverbs also states, "It is the glory of God to conceal a matter, but the glory of kings is to search out a matter" (25:2, NASB). God highlights the topic of generational curses all throughout Scripture to the person who has ears to hear what the Spirit is saying, and then He expects them to search out these clues until they solve a mystery of the kingdom.

> And he said unto them, Unto you it is given to know the mystery of the kingdom of God: but unto them that are without, all these things are done in parables.
>
> —MARK 4:11–13, KJV

This book is designed to help the reader collect the clues they've gathered all throughout the years and come to one conclusion: a Christian can have an active generational curse operating in their life through either ignorance, inheritance, or invitation. The work of redemption broke the power of the curse but did not eradicate its presence, just as the sacrifice of Jesus on the cross broke the power of sin but did not remove sin's presence. The apostle John tells us that even after salvation, believers will have moments during their journey of sanctification when they will sin, and they will be required not only to confess those sins and forsake them but also to allow God to *cleanse them* of all unrighteousness (1 John 1:9, KJV).

That phrase "cleanse us from all unrighteousness" is talking about finding the root cause of what is still giving sin its legal hold on a believer, causing the person to sin in that particular area. Most believers overlook that part of the verse by only focusing on "confess our sins," but the issue is twofold; we confess our sins, but we also allow God to cleanse us (break the curse; unrighteousness) of what's making us sin. The great news is that God not only will

remain faithful and just—which are courtroom terms—
in forgiving our sin but will also go a step further in helping us identify and cleanse ourselves from the curse that
empowers it.

In my first book, *The Secrets to Deliverance*, I explained
that for humans to have effective communication, the con-
cepts have to mean the same things for both parties, or
there will be a miscommunication as a result of *miscon-
ception*. This can be avoided by what I call "prototype tim-
ing." A prototype is an original model on which something
is patterned. Good communication requires finding the
right prototype that means the same thing to both parties. This is foundational in understanding the language of
deliverance, but generational curses require a different set
of rules of interpretation. This pearl of great price is hidden throughout Scripture in four ways: through *illustrations, shadows, figures,* and *mysteries*—and must be drawn
out from a determined seeker. Let's look at each one.

HIDDEN IN AN ILLUSTRATION

In Galatians, the apostle Paul gave us the greatest reference
point in being able to find hidden treasures in any field of
Scripture when he used the Greek word *állo*, which means
"other; different."[1] It is where we derive the word *allegory*, "a
story, poem, or picture in which there is another, hidden
meaning."[2] This opens up a whole new avenue of interpretation that allows God to highlight what's been hidden in
plain sight in understanding the secrets to the kingdom.

The greatest example of this can be found in Galatians

4:24, where Paul says that while Sarah (Abraham's wife) and Hagar (Abraham's concubine) were real people, their lives were illustrations, or allegories, of two covenants to be later revealed at the establishing of the new covenant. He goes on to explain that Hagar represents Mount Sinai, while her mistress, Sarah, represents the heavenly Jerusalem. Had Paul not pointed out the allegorical significance of these two women, their stories would be nothing more than historical information about Abraham's attempt to fulfill God's promise by trying to have a child with his concubine Hagar.

> These two women serve as an illustration of God's two covenants. The first woman, Hagar, represents Mount Sinai where people received the law that enslaved them. And now Jerusalem is just like Mount Sinai in Arabia, because she and her children live in slavery to the law. But the other woman, Sarah, represents the heavenly Jerusalem. She is the free woman, and she is our mother.
>
> —GALATIANS 4:24–26

Paul goes on to state that Sarah's role was more than that of just being Abraham's wife; her life is also connected to the spiritual DNA of all believers, just as Abraham is considered the father of faith. Paul says of Sarah, "She is our mother" (v. 26). This statement immediately shifts the text from a historical context to a spiritual one of honoring the heavenly Jerusalem. Exodus 20:12 tells us, "Honor your father and your *mother*" (ESV)—the only commandment with a promise attached to it. This promise is physical but also allegorical in that honoring your mother can produce a lasting inheritance of longevity on the earth.

When it comes to generational curses, you immediately find there are no scriptures using the term openly, but you find generational curses hidden in the extremely large field of biblical events, commandments, psalms, epistles, and prophecies in both the Old and New Testaments. Seeking out this treasure requires the reader to become more allegorical than literal. One of the downfalls of proper hermeneutics, or the proper interpretation of Scripture, is that it trains students to be trapped in "black letters on white pages" and doesn't allow them to view Scripture from an allegorical perspective. So when reading the story of Sarah and Hagar, you find nothing more than a story about two women married to one man. In proper exegesis, yes—this is what we're reading—but in an allegorical sense we're dealing with two covenants, and everything that is recorded in Scripture about the details of their lives has some spiritual significance in the life of the believer.

In the text we're told that Hagar represents Mount Sinai and that her spiritual DNA has been transferred to her spiritual bloodline: "she and her children live in slavery to the law" (Gal. 4:25). If this is not a perfect example of the generational curse of slavery being transferred (post-crucifixion) to her descendants, I don't know what is! This curse of slavery continues to exist four thousand years later to those blinded to the freedom that can only be found in Jesus Christ. Even after salvation many believers are still in bondage to legalism, keeping them from walking in the fullness of the generational blessing of Isaac, "the son of the freeborn wife [who] was born as God's own fulfillment of his promise" (v. 23).

Had Paul not been allegorical in his interpretation of this passage, we would never have known the story of Hagar and Sarah has a much deeper meaning. If this one story has great significance that could only be discovered through an allegorical approach, then how many more stories in Scripture have hidden allegorical meanings of both blessings and curses? We will explore many of them in the upcoming chapters.

HIDDEN IN A SHADOW

God told Moses to make sure that when he created the tabernacle, he used the blueprint—the exact pattern—shown to him on the mountain (Exod. 25:40). Everything had to be a 100 percent representation of what he saw because if it wasn't, it would cast a different shadow and produce a different meaning in the New Testament. This method of gaining more insight into the revelation of generational curses allows us to see the silhouette, or outline, of something— what the Bible calls a *shadow*.

A shadow is a form of an object that is cast by light. The Greek word *skia* means "an image cast by an object and representing the form of that object."[3] If I could define this word in one phrase it would be "the shadow represents." This word *shadow* appears two times in Hebrews to describe both the furnishing/functioning of the tabernacle and the hidden meanings to many of the laws stipulated by Moses. In Hebrews 8:4–5 we read, "If he were on earth, he would not be a priest, for there are already priests who offer the gifts prescribed by the law. They serve at a sanctuary that is a copy and *shadow* of what is in heaven." The author is letting us know that the tabernacle with all its furnishings, priesthood, and sacrifices was a shadow that represents something else—heaven's temple—which would later be revealed in the New Testament.

The next verse we will look at opens a new way of viewing the Law of Moses by saying it was a shadow. According to some scholars, Moses gave the children of Israel a total of 613 commandments. This opens up for us an inexhaustible opportunity to find at least 613 shadows of good things that were to come at a later dispensation. Let's read:

> The old system under the law of Moses was only a shadow, a dim preview of the good things to come, not the good things themselves.
>
> —HEBREWS 10:1

The text even goes on to say that the law itself was *not* the good thing. This is not saying the Law of Moses is obsolete for the believer but rather is fulfilled in Christ, who would come at a later time to do just that. But the commandments were a shadow, a form, of something that was coming to reveal their true meaning. The law was not a means to an end but pointed to Christ.

These verses from Hebrews help us recognize when the Scriptures are highlighting generational curses hidden as shadows within many biblical passages and stories. The

Scriptures take on a whole new meaning when you're not limited to black letters on white pages but are able to see revelation because of the form being cast by the illumination of the daystar rising behind it—and truths hidden before the foundation of the world suddenly get revealed. Maybe that's what the apostle Paul meant when he said,

> "No eye has seen, no ear has heard, and no mind
> has imagined what God has prepared for those
> who love him." But it was to us that God revealed
> these things by his Spirit. For his Spirit searches
> out everything and shows us God's deep secrets.
> —1 CORINTHIANS 2:9–10

Right now thank the Holy Spirit for choosing you to be one of those who can see, hear, and understand the deep things of God. Ask Him to increase your ability to see by highlighting every scripture where generational curses are hidden in a shadow and to sharpen your ability to hear so you'll be able to quickly recognize a generational curse when you hear it. Also ask the Spirit of God to enlarge your capacity to understand so you can receive new insight and fresh revelation about generational curses, in Jesus' name!

HIDDEN IN A FIGURE

Another method God uses to reveal hidden truths from Genesis to Revelation is through figures. The Greek word for *figures* is *typos*, from which we get the word *type*, meaning pattern, example, or prophetic symbol used to prefigure a future person.[4] Out of all the methods, this is the

THE SECRETS TO GENERATIONAL CURSES

one most widely used by God, as the personalities in the Scriptures can be used as a pattern for God-fearing behavior and also as a prophetic symbol of some revelation yet to be discovered.

Paul said in Romans 15:4 that whatever was written in the past was written for our learning, meaning the stories were literal events that happened but also patterns for us to follow in the New Testament.

An example of this can be found in the life of Abraham. We find God telling Pharaoh in Genesis 20:7, "Now return the man's wife, for he is a prophet, and he will pray for you and you will live. But if you do not return her, you may be sure that you and all who belong to you will die" (NIV). Why would God deal so severely with Pharaoh concerning Abraham when nowhere in the Scriptures does it record Abraham prophesying? His life was a *figure* and a prophetic symbol that would be used to prefigure not only God but also Christ and the church. Had Pharaoh disobeyed the voice of the Lord, it would have created a ripple effect that altered and rewrote the Scriptures' prophetic future. Every action Abraham was to take was a figure for our time now, in which he would become the spiritual father of both Jews and Gentiles.

> So the promise is received by faith. It is given as a free gift. And we are all certain to receive it, whether or not we live according to the law of Moses, if we have faith like Abraham's. For Abraham is the father of all who believe. That is what the Scriptures *mean* when God told him, "I have

made you the father of many nations." This happened because Abraham believed in the God who brings the dead back to life and who creates new things out of nothing.

—ROMANS 4:16–17

Now Abraham is just one biblical personality whose life and actions are a figure, or type. Many other biblical figures fall under the same category because their life choices produced consequences that are also types for the believer in modern times. This is where generational blessings and curses can also be seen in figures and types. If a Christian reading about these biblical personalities understands that they're figures, it will be easy to accept that generational curses—like generational blessings—fall into that category as well. In later chapters we will explore these figures more in depth and see how generational curses originate and operate even after the death, burial, and resurrection of Jesus Christ.

HIDDEN IN A MYSTERY

Jesus told His disciples in Matthew 13:11, "To you it has been given to know the secrets of the kingdom of heaven, but to them it has *not* been given" (ESV). In essence Jesus was saying that by grace He had personally bypassed the process of searching out clues by giving them the answer to the mystery directly. A mystery can be figured out by those willing to take the time to search out the clues, gather them, study them, and come to a definitive conclusion. Investigating a mystery requires time, patience, and careful attention to detail, plus following every lead (even if it leads to a dead end). The benefits of the kingdom are only available to those who seek for them. The clues are out there scattered in the field of Scripture waiting to be discovered.

There are multiple mysteries in the Word: the mystery of Christ (Rom. 16:25), the mystery of the wisdom of God (1 Cor. 2:7), the mystery of the resurrection (1 Cor. 15:51), the mystery of God's will (Eph. 1:9), the mystery of Christ and the church (Eph. 5:32), and the *mystery of iniquity* (2 Thess. 2:7, KJV), which we will cover in depth in the upcoming chapters. No one talked more about the mysteries of the kingdom than the apostle Paul. It was his desire that the church, both Jew and Gentile, would understand all mysteries hidden since the foundation of the world. Paul didn't want us to remain ignorant that Christ died to give us access to understanding the kingdom if we would search for it by paying close attention to the clues. He said, "I do not want you to be *ignorant of this mystery*...so that you may not be conceited" (Rom. 11:25, NIV).

Finding generational curses outlined in the Scriptures requires careful searching and paying attention to clues attached to the mystery of iniquity. But the great news is that we have a promise from the Lord and Paul that those who pay the price to seek after the kingdom will have eyes to see and ears to hear the deep things of God.

When using these four methods—illustrations, shadows, figures, and mysteries—in your Scripture-reading paradigm, you'll discover the hidden secrets of the kingdom without crossing boundaries into doctrinal error. You'll be able to understand some of the simplest statements Jesus made, such as "you must be born again," and not be trapped, assuming that a man can actually go back into his mother's womb. You'll be able to explore difficult topics and see with clarity subjects such as generational curses, demons, and deliverance. Our heavenly Father rejoices in revealing such truth to those who really want to know. He takes pleasure in revealing the secrets of generational curses so you can identify and break some of the most hidden curses from being transferred generation to generation in your household.

The generational curse can be broken, and both you and your household can be set free! Jesus Christ holds the keys to every bloodline and can open prison doors and set the captives free. Pray this prayer with me right now, asking the Holy Spirit to broaden your perspective of the Scriptures by incorporating these four keys into your theological framework and paradigm.

> *Holy Spirit, You are the Spirit of truth, and it's through You the holy Scriptures were inspired and written. You are the author of revelation. I ask You to remove all blinders, veils, and scales over my understanding and recalibrate my understanding as I read Your Word. Holy teacher, give me the spirit of wisdom and insight into heaven's illustrations, shadows, figures, and mysteries of the kingdom hidden all throughout the Scriptures. As I read this book, reveal to me where I have generational curses operating in my life, and show me the strategy to deactivate and remove them. Lord*

> Jesus, thank You for setting me free and showing
> me how to remain free from every curse. In Your
> name I pray, amen.

THE WEAPON OF MISINFORMATION

Before we go any further in uncovering generational curses,
we must first address the misinformation surrounding
them. To be clear, misinformation is false or incorrect
information that is spread intentionally or unintentionally.
Of all the enemies to the revelation of generational curses,
misinformation reigns as its archnemesis. And there is
more misinformation out there about curses than there is
anti-curses propaganda.

As I travel the country, I spend more time correcting
misinformation than actually conducting deliverance. I
find myself having to correct the errors of what the church
believes generational curses to be or not be before helping
any church go through mass deliverance. All misinformation must be addressed and eradicated before generational
curses can be dismantled. Misinformation's sole purpose
has always been one thing: to get the church in error.

> Jesus replied, "You are in *error* because you do not
> know the Scriptures or the power of God."
> —MATTHEW 22:29, NIV

Being in *error* is more dangerous than being in false doctrine. When a church is in false doctrine, everyone knows
it because the church at large has been trained to recognize
and reject heresy. But when a church is in error, they don't

know it and can't figure out why true doctrine is not working for them. Error is having sound doctrine but not understanding the essence of why it was said, therefore producing no manifestation of that truth.

The rejection of generational curses is more modern than ancient. The early church believed in demons, deliverance, and generational curses and regularly practiced the ministry of deliverance for both nonbelievers and believers. What I have found in my travels is that 99 percent of misinformation about generational curses is being perpetuated by sincere believers (some theologians) seeking to help the church walk in the fullness of Christ by removing the preoccupation of those who blame everything on demons and curses and never take any personal responsibility for their habitual patterns of sinful behavior. I haven't found one person spreading misinformation on this topic with malicious intent; instead everyone I encounter has a sincere desire to help the church. Unfortunately, it doesn't make it any more helpful but actually perpetuates what I call "fake news" about generational curses. And as in real life, most people would rather assume that fake news is real than investigate the facts and come to the truthful conclusion.

Though many examples of misinformation are circulating in the body of Christ about why a believer can't have an active generational curse in their life (after the crucifixion), I've narrowed the list down to these top four: (1) Jesus became the curse, (2) Christians can only have generational blessings, (3) sins of the parents, and (4) "neither his sins nor his parents' sins." They represent the arguments used most frequently in debate.

JESUS BECAME THE CURSE

"Jesus became the curse!" If you haven't heard this argument for the improbability of a believer having a generational curse "after the cross," then you haven't been studying or discussing this topic long enough, because it's probably the number one biblical argument used by sincere believers—but it's misinformation. It comes directly from Galatians 3:13 (ESV):

> Christ redeemed us from the curse of the law by *becoming* a curse for us—for it is written, "Cursed is everyone who is hanged on a tree."

Most believers quote this verse as proof that it's impossible for a Christian to have a generational curse, because the Greek word for *become* is *ginomai*, which means to be made, finished, accomplished, breaking.[5] The assumption is that if Jesus *became* the curse, then the curse no longer exists, therefore making it unscriptural to insist that a Christian can have a curse active in their life. The only problem with this line of thinking is that the word *ginomai* (become) also appears in the following two passages. Let's look at the first.

> For our sake he made him to be sin who knew no sin, so that in him we might *become* the righteousness of God.
>
> —2 CORINTHIANS 5:21, ESV

If we continue with this line of thinking—that the word *became* means to completely remove, finish, or exchange—that would mean Christ's work on the cross should have also completely removed the sin because He *became* sin. But this is not the case because it directly contradicts 1 John 1:8, which clearly states that the presence of sin has not been eradicated for the believer and to make such a claim would actually mean we are in deception. Let's read:

> If we say that we have no sin, we deceive ourselves, and the truth is not in us.
>
> —1 JOHN 1:8

The apostle John and the early church were aware that the presence of sin had not been eradicated but rather its power and authority over a believer had been broken through the finished work of Christ on the cross. John was so convinced the believer still sins even after receiving Jesus Christ as Savior that he goes on to say that the need for daily confession of sin *as a Christian* is needed. He even goes a step further by identifying the need to break the curse giving that sin legal grounds.

> If we confess our sins, he is faithful and just to forgive us our sins, and to cleanse us from all unrighteousness.
>
> —1 JOHN 1:9, KJV

The phrase "cleanse us from all unrighteousness" is in direct reference to identifying the source that gives a particular sin its legal grounds in our lives and being cleansed (through deliverance) from it. This is not just "confess your daily sin" but also find the root that empowers it and be cleansed from it as well. The phrase "all unrighteousness" is also interchangeable with the word *iniquity,* so the verse should really read like this: "cleanse us from all iniquity."

The verse goes on, saying in verse 10, "if we say that we have not sinned, we make him a liar, and his word is not in us" (KJV). This verse is not talking about pre-crucifixion, because it is the concluding thought in direct connection to the previous two verses, where believers are required to daily get cleansed from sin through daily confession and repentance. The key phrase in this verse is "we make him a liar." This lets us know it is *God* advising us that the crucifixion of Jesus Christ broke the power of sin but not its presence—just as the work of redemption also broke the power of the curse but not its presence.

The great news is that a time is coming in the near future when the presence of sin, death, hell, demons, the devil, and every generational curse will be completely annihilated and swallowed up in victory! First Corinthians 15:54 says, "So when this corruptible shall have put on incorruption, and this mortal shall have put on immortality, then shall be brought to pass the saying that is written, Death is swallowed up in victory" (KJV).

If you're reading this, you don't have to be the slave of secret sin (no matter how vile); neither do you have to be the prisoner of a generational curse. You can be free, and the power of that curse can be legally stopped by applying the truths outlined in this book.

CHRISTIANS CAN ONLY HAVE GENERATIONAL BLESSINGS

If you've been in the church for quite some time, you've probably heard numerous sermons, teachings, and conferences stating, "We believe in generational blessings but not generational curses." To understand this next argument will require one to understand the law of dualism in Scripture. God uses dualism to validate the authenticity of something. All throughout Scripture you find this dualistic concept to help validate its opposite. Nothing can be authenticated if its opposite isn't present to contrast it.

The story of the two prostitutes looking to settle a dispute with King Solomon concerning a dead child is a clear example of this. The story, found in 1 Kings chapter 3, narrates that both prostitutes have children; then one child dies, and during the night its mother switches the dead child for the live one. Upon waking up the next morning, the mother of the living child realizes the baby isn't hers, and the women present the case to Solomon, who is a newly installed king. Both prostitutes argue their cases and are very convincing.

In a display of divine wisdom, King Solomon commands that a sword be brought and the child be cut in two, giving one half to each mother. The child's real mother relinquishes her fight and hands the child to the mother of the dead baby in hopes of keeping her baby alive, therefore revealing who the child's real mother is. For a true mother's love will prefer to keep her child alive than kill him. We find this dualism all over Scripture, beginning with when

19

God created the heavens and the earth and separated the night from the day (Gen. 1).

- Jesus said He would prefer you to be hot or cold: "I know all the things you do, that you are neither hot nor cold. I wish that you were one or the other!" (Rev. 3:15).

- Death and life are in the power of the tongue: "The tongue has the power of life and death, and those who love it will eat its fruit" (Prov. 18:21, NIV).

- Moses said, "I set before you life and death": "Today I have given you the choice between life and death, between blessings and curses. Now I call on heaven and earth to witness the choice you make. Oh, that you would choose life, so that you and your descendants might live!" (Deut. 30:19).

Even in many of the parables Jesus shared you find dualism appearing multiple times: for a father had two sons, one who did his father's will and the other who didn't (Matt. 21:28–32); the widow gave two coins (Mark 12:41–44).

How does this dualism relate to generational curses and specifically to generational blessings? Simple: generational blessings cannot be validated without the presence of generational curses. Its contrast and counterpart reveal and verify its authenticity and existence. If you remove the presence of generational curses, then generational blessings don't have a contrast to authenticate them. We wouldn't know what the blessing is if there wasn't a curse to compare and contrast it to.

Time wouldn't allow me to go further in explaining this point, but there are multitudes of references: heaven and hell, Old Testament and New Testament, tree of life and tree of the knowledge of good and evil, and so forth. So when I hear the church declare that they receive generational blessings but completely reject the idea of generational curses, it's clear that sound biblical understanding might be lacking or faulty. They haven't really considered proper exegesis concerning the dualism of Scripture.

The good news is that you don't have to fear losing your generational blessing to a curse because you're seated with Christ in heavenly places (Eph. 2:6), and from that place of authority the devil, demons, and curses have been stripped of their power, and at the end of the age their presence will be completely eradicated by Jesus Christ. Take a few moments right now and thank the Lord for His wonderful work on Calvary in nailing our defeat, shame, sickness, and every curse to His cross.

SINS OF THE PARENTS (SHARING IN THE GUILT)

This third argument against generational curses gains its false footing in the following verse, which records a statement God made to the prophet Ezekiel:

> The one who sins is the one who will die. The
> child will not share the guilt of the parent, nor
> will the parent share the guilt of the child. The
> righteousness of the righteous will be credited to
> them, and the wickedness of the wicked will be
> charged against them.
>
> —Ezekiel 18:20, NIV

To properly understand this verse, one has to consider the context of the rest of the chapter and the other statements made leading up to it. God was confronting the Israelites' views concerning personal responsibility for sin and the shifting of blame for irresponsible behavior. Since the Garden of Eden humankind has been making excuses for sin by blame-shifting. We find Adam blaming Eve, then Eve blaming the serpent, and up until today humankind (including believers) still refuses to take personal responsibility for years of iniquity. The excuses are endless in blaming others for our lack of constraint in fulfilling our own personal desires. Several Bible translations even call it our own "lust."

> But each person is tempted when they are
> dragged away by their *own* desires and enticed.
> Then, when desire has conceived, it gives birth to
> sin; and sin, when it is full-grown, brings forth
> death.
>
> —James 1:14–15, NKJV

Shifting the blame eases the conscience of feeling the severity of our sins. Keep in mind that during the time of

Ezekiel the Israelites were under the judgment of God that would last for seventy years of exile in the land of Mesopotamia. During the exile many children were born under Babylonian rule, and the following phrase became a proverb among the Israelites as they watched their innocent children being born under cruel bondage:

> The parents eat sour grapes, and the children's teeth are set on edge.
>
> —Ezekiel 18:2, NIV

This proverb was a way to explain their present suffering during the Babylonian exile. The phrase "teeth are set on edge" describes a bad taste left in your mouth or refers to something unpleasant and annoying. That statement had some validity because the seventy-year captivity was the direct result of the willful sins of their ancestors, but ultimately everyone is held accountable for their own sins. An improper exegesis of the text assumes the Lord is saying children are held responsible for the sins of their parents, but if you look closely at verse 20 you'll see one word God is emphasizing that most overlook: *guilt*!

> The child will not share the *guilt* of the parent, nor will the parent share the *guilt* of the child. The righteousness of the righteous will be credited to them, and the wickedness of the wicked will be charged against them.
>
> —Ezekiel 18:20, NIV

What God was actually saying is that children will not be held guilty by the courtroom of heaven's legal system, or by the Law of Moses, for the transgressions committed by their ancestors. Many of those transgressions required capital punishment of death by stoning. God, who is righteous, just, and true, would never hold anyone guilty for a transgression they did not commit. He said in Ezekiel 18:4, "The soul that sinneth, it shall die" (KJV), meaning that everyone will be held responsible and suffer the consequences of their own sinful behavior. But God never said He would protect you from the predisposition toward those sins and curses. The issue of generational curses is *not* a question of suffering the penalty of the sins committed by your forefathers; it's about being born genetically predisposed to those sins because the root has been transferred down. (We will get into more detail about this in the upcoming chapter.)

A person can indeed be born inclined toward a particular sin placed there through a process called "epigenetic modification" in the scientific world—in other words, through the iniquity being passed down to the third and fourth generations.[6] That's why the Bible calls it the *mystery* of iniquity (2 Thess. 2:7, KJV)!

To further drive this point, there is a huge misunderstanding in the argument that generational curses refer to falling under the judgment of previous sins committed by our parents. The following verse is a clear indication that to do so would be unjust by the courtroom of heaven and the Law of Moses. Let's read:

> When Amaziah was well established as king, he executed the officials who had assassinated his father. However, he did not kill the children of the assassins, for he obeyed the command of the LORD as written by Moses in the Book of the Law: "Parents must not be put to death for the sins of their children, nor children for the sins of their parents. Those deserving to die must be put to death for their own crimes."
>
> —2 KINGS 14:5–6

A generational curse is the predisposition and inclination toward a particular sin that is passed down within the bloodline upon birth. David said, "I was shapen in iniquity" (Ps. 51:5, KJV). This book is designed to help you put the clues together and solve the mystery of iniquity in your own family bloodline and then break those generational curses by the efficacy of Christ's work on the cross. Jesus is the curse breaker!

No matter if you were born into iniquity or are feeling the effects of your own transgressions, call on the Holy Spirit right now and ask Him to reveal the root of your iniquity—and proceed to break the curse.

JESUS PROVED THERE ARE NO CURSES

The fourth argument that's gaining momentum can be found in John 9 concerning the man born blind. Let's read:

> As Jesus was walking along, he saw a man who had been blind from birth. "Rabbi," his disciples

> asked him, "why was this man born blind? Was it
> because of his own sins or his parents' sins?"
>
> "It was *not* because of his sins or his parents'
> sins," Jesus answered.
>
> —JOHN 9:1–3

The antagonists against generational curses will zealously affirm that here Jesus was indicating that such curses don't play a role in the misfortunes of human civilization by stating that this man's blindness was *not* the result of his sins or ancestral curses. They improperly exegete Jesus' statement as a decree for all humans everywhere but fail to read the verses that follow, where Jesus specifies that heaven had been orchestrating this man's blindness from the beginning and would use his healing as a great witness that Jesus was the Messiah.

> This happened so the power of God could be seen
> in him. We must quickly carry out the tasks
> assigned us by the one who sent us. The night is
> coming, and then no one can work.
>
> —JOHN 9:3–4

This man's blindness was allowed for one purpose only: so that the power of God could be on full display in Jesus' healing him and that this man would be a foreshadowing of every human born spiritually blind and in desperate need of the light of the glorious gospel of Jesus Christ. Jesus' declaration was isolated to this man's life and not a universal decree for human civilization concerning generational curses.

CONCLUDING THOUGHTS

Dealing with generational curses is like going to court during a trial. Most trial cases aren't dealt with at the moment of arrest, but those arrested are given a future date on which their case will go to trial. Well today, as you read this book, your bloodline is on trial, but the great news is that Jesus is our Advocate (lawyer), and He wins every case! The work that Jesus did on the cross for you resolved all curses against you and your bloodline! As you read the prayers in this book, just know that every curse will be broken and defeated in your life. Your trial ends with the Judge saying, "You are free, and free indeed—case closed."

Now that we laid the groundwork for reading the rest of this book, let's take a few moments and ask the Holy Spirit to continue shaping our worldview concerning this topic of generational curses. Let's ask Him to reveal the deepest and most hidden curses that might be hindering us from growing to our fullest potential in Christ as we move through this book. Let's pray.

> Holy Spirit, You are the great revealer of the secrets of men's hearts and the illuminator of heaven's truths. I ask You to broaden and expand my capacity of understanding the secrets of the kingdom. Grant me the insight and knowledge of generational curses in all wisdom and spiritual understanding. Reveal in me every generational curse at work hidden deep within my body and bloodline. Jesus, I ask You to annul every

legal right that the devil may have over my life and bloodline through iniquity and curses. Heavenly Father, I ask for Your guidance, and may the courtroom of heaven grant me strength as I proclaim the declarations outlined in the pages of this book, in Jesus' name!

CHAPTER 2

HUMAN WIRING AND EPIGENETICS

These are the generations of Noah: Noah was a just man and perfect in his generations, and Noah walked with God.

—GENESIS 6:9, KJV

Behold, *I was shapen* in iniquity; and in sin did my mother conceive me.

—PSALM 51:5, KJV

Among them we too all formerly lived in the lusts of our flesh, indulging the desires of the flesh and of the mind, and *were by nature* children of wrath, even as the rest.

—EPHESIANS 2:3, NASB95

HUMAN PURPOSE AND THE COURTROOM

Before we take a deep dive into the topic of generational curses, it is necessary to explain the courtroom of heaven's role in the creation of humankind and the current role it plays all throughout a person's life until death. Every person's life, purpose, destiny, geographical location, talents, family, exact day of death, and so forth have all been pre-ordained by the courtroom of heaven. This is why when a person dies, that very same courtroom will call them into account concerning their life lived on the earth. A couple of factors are at work before a person is actually conceived in the womb. Each life born on earth is not just the result of two humans coming together through intimacy and conceiving another life. A whole system is at work in the heavens for that conception to be made possible. That is why human life is precious to God and the heavenly council that helps Him govern the universe.

First there is what the Bible calls *foreknowing*, which means God in His foreknowledge decided within Himself (with no outside influence) what each human would look like, what personality they would have, what gender and character traits they would have, and so on. Once He foreknows, He *predestines*, which means He decides what destiny or role this person will play in fulfilling His sovereign will on the earth.

> For those God foreknew he also predestined to be conformed to the image of his Son, that he might be the firstborn among many brothers and sisters.
> —ROMANS 8:29, NIV

Once God has predestined, the council of the heavenly court is allowed to get involved in the logistics of how God's sovereign plan for this person will be carried out. The Bible tells us that after God's will is determined in heaven, a human "body" is assigned.

> Wherefore when he cometh into the world, he saith, Sacrifice and offering thou wouldest not, but *a body* hast thou prepared me....Then said I,

> Lo, I come (in the volume of the book it is written
> of me,) to do thy will, O God.
>
> —HEBREWS 10:5, 7, KJV

Even though this passage is talking specifically about Jesus, the phrase "a body hast thou prepared me" applies to all human beings. Notice how God's will is determined before a body is assigned. Once a body is assigned, the person is born in this world already *ordained* to carry out God's purpose. We see this in the birth of Jeremiah.

> Then the word of the LORD came unto me, say-
> ing, Before I formed thee in the belly I knew thee;
> and before thou camest forth out of the womb
> I sanctified thee, and I *ordained* thee a prophet
> unto the nations.
>
> —JEREMIAH 1:4–5, KJV

Here's another verse clearly outlining God's will over a person's birth. We just visited this passage in the last chapter (in our list of arguments against generational curses), but here I want you to pay special attention to the last sentence.

> As Jesus was walking along, he saw a man who
> had been blind from birth. "Rabbi," his disciples
> asked him, "why was this man born blind? Was it
> because of his own sins or his parents' sins?"
>
> "It was not because of his sins or his parents'
> sins," Jesus answered. "*This happened so the power
> of God could be seen in him.*"
>
> —JOHN 9:1–3

Now I'm sharing all this because before we begin to understand generational curses and their effect on human life, we have to see humankind's origin and connection to the courtroom of heaven. Generational curses originate in the courtroom of heaven (Ps. 82:1–3—we will discuss this further in other chapters).

"I WAS SHAPEN IN INIQUITY"

Now that we understand the courtroom of heaven's role in human life, the following verses will begin to make sense, and we will understand why David said that he was shaped in iniquity in the womb.

> Behold, I was shapen in iniquity; and in sin did my mother conceive me.
>
> —PSALM 51:5, KJV

Let me start off by saying there is a lot to unpack in this verse. Many theologians suggest this statement from David is more than just a declaration that all humans are born in sin; it also refers to the origin of David's conception. Many theologians and seminaries teach that David was likely conceived as the result of an adulterous affair (plausible, not absolute). It is assumed that when the prophet Samuel asked Jesse if he had any more sons, it was because Jesse was trying to conceal David's existence.

> So he asked Jesse, "Are these all the sons you have?"
>
> "There is still the youngest," Jesse answered.

"He is tending the sheep." Samuel said, "Send for
him; we will not sit down until he arrives."
—1 SAMUEL 16:11, NIV

This is also the reason why when David won favor with
King Saul and was offered the king's daughter in marriage,
he referred to his family as the lowest among all the tribes
of Judah. His pessimism was deeply entrenched because
of a secret past. (This is all theological speculation among
theologians, but food for thought.)

"Who am I, and what is my family in Israel
that I should be the king's son-in-law?" David
exclaimed. "My father's family is nothing!"
—1 SAMUEL 18:18

Looking at the story of David's birth from this plausible perspective sheds a bit more light on why David would
state in Psalm 51 that he was shaped in iniquity, and "in
sin" did his mother conceive him (not as in "born in sin"
because of Adam, but as in willful transgression, or not
within the confines of marriage). Is what I'm saying far-
fetched? Possibly. But this narrative is common in Jewish
tradition according to the Babylonian Talmud (*Bava Batra*
91a). Feel free to look it up.

David is basically saying the potential controversy surrounding his conception is the root cause of his proclivities. When people are suffering from an identity crisis, it's
usually rooted in something surrounding their birth or
the reasons for their conception. You will often hear the

famous phrase, "I was born this way." Let's analyze that more closely.

Epigenetic Modification: I Was Born This Way

In the last couple of years there have been some scientific discoveries to verify that it's genetically possible that people are "born this way," meaning born genetically predisposed toward a particular pattern of behavior that was inherited by a previous generation, which they have no control over. Especially within the science of gender identity. When this news first hit, it was met with much skepticism by both the scientific community and the church. But in recent years, through more research, it has been scientifically proven that a person can indeed be "born this way." My own personal view has also evolved in the area according to the Bible verse we find here:

> Behold, I was shapen in iniquity; and in sin did my mother conceive me.
> —Psalm 51:5, KJV

If a person is shaped in iniquity, then the question to ask is, Where did those iniquities come from? The text doesn't say "I was shaped in sin"; if so it would readily mean the sin of Adam that was passed down to all who are born on this earth. But it says *iniquity*. This category of sin is a bit more personal. Iniquity is personal transgression committed over long periods of time in which a person has the potential to have their DNA altered toward a particular sin. They go from doing this sin to actually embodying it! It would make sense that under the right conditions a person can activate those iniquities.

WHAT IS EPIGENETIC MODIFICATION?

Epigenetic modifications are modifications to DNA that regulate whether genes are turned on or off. These modifications are attached to DNA and do not change the sequence of DNA building blocks but give it information about how to behave.

Did you just read that part? *Give it information about how to behave.* Have you ever heard someone say, "I just couldn't help myself," or, "I was born this way"? Well, maybe they couldn't help themselves, and *maybe* (notice I said maybe) they were indeed born that way—because the information to behave in that manner was already deposited in them through hereditary information! Because of this, my view of "I was born this way" has changed in recent years. I'm beginning to think that people indeed *are* born that way, and now it makes a bit more sense why Jesus said you must be "born again," because if epigenetic modification (also known as hereditary sin) is a real thing and a person is "born this way," then it must be broken through salvation by the regenerative power of the Holy Spirit.

The Bible says that Noah was perfect in his GENErations—meaning that his bloodline was free from any epigenetic modification, and I know he received it from his great-grandfather Enoch. The Bible says that Enoch walked so closely with God that God took him (Gen. 5).

Enoch's DNA was so full of God that his son Methuselah became the oldest person who ever lived. Three generations later, a man named Lamech gave birth to a son and called him Noah, and the rest is history.

This is why when you visit a medical clinic for the first time, they make you fill out paperwork with questions about your background. Why is this done? The doctor doesn't want to have to guess what's wrong with you, and knowing your background helps him or her better assess your current illness. He wants to see what genetic makeup is within your bloodline and which sicknesses have been frequent. The same could be said about sin and curses. Through discernment the Holy Spirit can show you which information is being transferred from one generation to the next—or rather which lies the enemy has caused your family to believe, which judgment and curse from heaven is being enforced. Sometimes when you meet people, you can just sense either the blessing of the Lord on them or a curse.

> The LORD curses the *house* of the wicked, but he
> blesses the *home* of the upright.
> —PROVERBS 3:33

In the coming chapters we will thoroughly flesh this out to help you better understand where you might need to do some "housecleaning" and also where you might need to do some enforcing.

CURSES FROM BOTH SIDES
OF THE FAMILY

A perfect example of potential epigenetic modification can be found in the life of John the Baptist and his parents, Zechariah and Elizabeth. Luke chapter 1 narrates the announcement of his birth by the angel Gabriel and the future and lifestyle John would have. We find his mother already old in age and well beyond the age of childbearing. Now with child, she recluses herself away from public scrutiny for the whole term of her pregnancy, so much so that Gabriel tells her cousin Mary (mother of Jesus) to go visit her to console her.

> Soon afterward his wife, Elizabeth, became pregnant and went into seclusion for five months.
> —LUKE 1:24

But it was too late. The damage had been done, as we find that just as Elizabeth struggled with isolation, so we see her son John isolated in the wilderness during his earthly ministry.

> John grew up and became strong in spirit. And he lived in the wilderness until he began his public ministry to Israel.
> —LUKE 1:80

Instead of evangelizing from town to town like his cousin Jesus, you find John secluded away from the public, in the desert—just like his mother, Elizabeth. And it didn't end there. We find another curse coming down the bloodline through his father, Zechariah, dealing with doubt during his dialogue with the angel:

> Zechariah said to the angel, "How can I be sure
> this will happen? I'm an old man now, and my
> wife is also well along in years." Then the angel
> said, "I am Gabriel! I stand in the very presence
> of God. It was he who sent me to bring you this
> good news! But now, since you didn't believe what
> I said, you will be silent and unable to speak until
> the child is born. For my words will certainly be
> fulfilled at the proper time."
>
> —LUKE 1:18–20

And we also find John doubting his proclamation that Jesus was the Lamb of God. While in prison he sent his disciples to ask Jesus if He really was the Christ. Read the following verses:

> John the Baptist, who was in prison, heard about
> all the things the Messiah was doing. So he sent
> his disciples to ask Jesus, "Are you the Messiah
> we've been expecting, or should we keep looking
> for someone else?"
>
> —MATTHEW 11:2–3

We see that John's unbelief was passed down to him by his father, Zechariah, and his isolated personality was passed down to him by his mother.

CURSES WIRED TO YOUR LAST NAME?

> Lamech's other wife, Zillah, gave birth to a son named Tubal-cain. He became an expert in forging tools of bronze and iron. Tubal-cain had a sister named Naamah.
>
> —GENESIS 4:22

As you can see from this text, this is the first time in Scripture where a first and last name are used. A name carried the weight of what the name means, along with the actions (both good and bad) of the persons who carried the name. In no other place in Scripture do we find the idea of epigenetic modification and transfer in the bloodline through a name. Let's look at the Hebrew name meanings.

Tubal: "the earth; the world; confusion"[1]

Cain: "possession, or possessed"[2]

Because Hebrew names have meaning as to the present and future destiny of the person, this is how it should be read when you merge both names: possessed with the world, confusion, and being earthly. If the name Tubal-cain isn't a clear depiction of a human soul devoid of God, totally given over to the sensuality and passions of this world, then I don't know what is. If you read more into the text you will find that Tubal-cain's name leads him to be the father of *weaponry*. Where did that intuition and discovery come from? It came from generations earlier through his great-great-great-great-grandfather Cain, who forged a weapon to kill his brother Abel. It only makes sense that that information was traveling down the bloodline.

> Lamech's other wife, Zillah, gave birth to a son
> named Tubal-cain. He became an expert in forg-
> ing tools of *bronze* and *iron* [weapons]. Tubal-cain
> had a sister named Naamah.
>
> —GENESIS 4:22

To assume that Lamech gave his son this name because he loved the sound of it—as many in our present generation do—would be a mistake. No, this name was given to Tubal-cain on purpose and with intent. Through epigenetics Tubal-cain would carry the genetic code of what his ancestor had done years earlier and cause it to evolve. We will get into how sin and curses evolve in chapter 5.

WIRED FROM BIRTH (GOLIATH)

Many people are genetically predisposed to particular things. The scientific evidence is clear. Epigenetic modification has shown that people can be born with information already deposited in their genes; this process makes it easier to continue certain patterns of behavior. It also explains why a young child can act, talk, and walk like some deceased family member they never met, but if that person is genetically close enough to the child, that information is readily available.

> "Don't be ridiculous!" Saul replied. "There's no way
> you can fight this Philistine and possibly win!
> You're only a boy, and he's been a man of war
> since his youth."
>
> —1 SAMUEL 17:33

The text says that Goliath was wired from his youth for war and battle. This made war and battling easier for him because he was born already having a warrior in him. It was easy for him to challenge the children of Israel to a fight because all he knew was fighting, no different from folks who only know how to sin—all they know is fornicating, all they know is the sinful lifestyle passed down to them.

Everyone is born with this wiring already deposited in them. These deposits are called "treasures," and this is what Jesus meant when He said, "Store up for yourselves treasures in heaven" (Matt. 6:20, NIV). Jesus wasn't talking about money, because we don't need money in heaven. He was talking about deposits of lifestyle, good deeds, and so on. It all gets stored up to be distributed for your future generations. Why? Because this same principle can be applied to generational blessings. Some people are born into families that love and honor God, and you see just how different their families turn out. Peace, joy, blessing, and favor seem to be their portion.

If you're reading this right now and feel like you're under a generational curse, you can turn that around! You can open a new heavenly bank account and begin to make deposits that can change the destiny of your bloodline. Heaven desires to bless you.

> The LORD is merciful and compassionate, slow to get angry and filled with unfailing love. The LORD is good to everyone. He showers compassion on all his creation.
>
> —PSALM 145:8–9

Being wired with information makes it easy to walk in the footsteps of a previous generation.

THE FOOTSTEPS

Footstep: a track; the mark or impression of the foot; token; mark; visible sign of a course pursued; as the footsteps of divine wisdom (Ps. 78:4).

> What sorrow awaits them! For they follow in the *footsteps* of Cain, who killed his brother. Like Balaam, they deceive people for money. And like Korah, they perish in their rebellion.
>
> —JUDE 11

We find in this text three biblical figures who, though alive during various times in Israel's history, are still plaguing the church today. How can Balaam's deception cause the prophets of today to chase after greed and prophesy divination? How can Cain, born during the dawn of human civilization, still cause humans to hate and kill each other? Korah's rebellion came during the time of Moses, and yet pastors, leaders, and churches thirty-five hundred years later are still dealing with rebellion within the leadership of the church. These biblical figures are long gone, but their "footsteps" still linger through the same demonic strongholds that inspired such behavior and are still causing humans—Christians included—to pass that information from generation to generation.

The spirit and functioning (attitude and impartation) are embedded in the footsteps, which is why it was the custom in the Old Testament for students to ask for a double portion of the spirit of the rabbi training them. We see this in the story of Elisha's request to his mentor, Elijah.

Footsteps predetermined the outcome of one's life.

> We can make our plans, but the LORD determines our [foot]steps.
>
> —PROVERBS 16:9

These footsteps are already deposited into our bloodline (genes) upon birth, and they predetermine the walk we will carry out later. God told Jeremiah that before he was born, He already deposited into his bloodline the office of the prophet, so in essence Jeremiah was "born this way." His path in life was already outlined, his divine ability to prophesy was already imparted into his spirit, but Jeremiah went a step further and said that the prophetic word of the Lord was like "fire in my bones!" (Jer. 20:9). He was left with no choice but to be who he was born to be.

An enormous amount of Scripture indicates that, yes indeed, humans are born with their genes predisposed to either good or evil. Eventually I reconsidered my position and now lean toward believing that "born this way" is biblically possible and may even be the reason why Jesus said, "Ye must be born again" (John 3:7, KJV).

FAITH AND BLESSING CAN BE INHERITED

Here is another example of how children can be born genetically empowered to move in a certain direction. As you can see from the text below, Timothy was able to move in the dimension of faith he did because it was in his bloodline. His mother walked by faith, along with his grandmother. The apostle Paul saw this and pointed it out to him in his epistle to the young pastor. This pedigree of faith was what helped Paul discern that Timothy could not just serve as a pastor of a local fellowship, though being young in age, but that he was also to become Paul's spiritual son in the faith.

> I am filled with joy as I think of your strong faith
> that was passed down through your family line. It
> began with your grandmother Lois, who passed it
> on to your dear mother, Eunice. And it's clear that
> you too are following in the footsteps of their godly
> example.
>
> —2 TIMOTHY 1:4–5, TPT

The whole revelation of spiritual paternity, or embracing your spiritual father and mother, is not about control; it's about spiritual DNA, inheritance, and legacy. It's about receiving spiritual resources from someone who's already paved the way and can help you reach your fullest potential in Christ. They can teach you how to surrender to Christ. They can model what it's like to spend hours in prayer seeking God. They can display Christlike character during times of suffering for the cause of Christ. They can instill in you the honor of total surrender to Scripture. Generational blessing can open doors for you that normally would take years to walk through. Someone already obtained it for you. Someone pioneered it for you. Someone nurtured it for you. Ask the Holy Spirit right now to show you where the generational blessing is coming from, and make it your business to never lose it!

PRAYER OF BLESSING

Heavenly Father, I thank You that You're a God of generations—the God of Abraham, Isaac, and Jacob! I ask that You teach me how to live for You so that Your presence can dwell in my family for all generations. Holy Spirit, thank You for guiding me into all truth. I will present my life blameless before the Lord. In Jesus' name.

KICKING ABOUT IN YOUR OWN BLOOD

Ezekiel chapter 16 gives the best description and revelation concerning generational curses of any place in Scripture. I never would have made the connection if the Holy Spirit hadn't highlighted it to me during my daily devotions one day.

Let's first describe what was happening when Ezekiel wrote this. Israel was in Babylonian captivity because God had exhausted all His mercy toward them after King Manasseh plunged the nation into fifty-two years of the most detestable idolatry Israel had ever seen. The prophet Jeremiah had prophesied that the nation would be sent into captivity for seventy years under the disciplining hand of God. While various prophets began to hear the word of the Lord, no one heard and saw into the dimension of the Spirit more than Ezekiel.

The text doesn't say this, but as with any prophets living during the time of judgment, there would be sincere prayers asking God "Why?" and what led to the captivity. The Lord gave him an answer—and it was more than Ezekiel could handle. I'm sure Ezekiel didn't fully understand what he saw, and he was probably thinking in natural terms, but for us New Testament believers the Holy Spirit provides a deeper meaning (without getting sensational and erroneous with the text). God showed Ezekiel the root cause of Israel's consistent rebellion and entrenched idolatry. Please read the following passage from an allegorical and typological lens. In the passage's proper exegesis, the Lord is talking about Israel. But you can also see a dual revelation in how God deals with all humans that are born into the world.

> Give her this message from the Sovereign LORD:
> You are nothing but a Canaanite! Your father was
> an Amorite and your mother a Hittite. On the
> day you were born, no one cared about you. Your
> umbilical cord was not cut, and you were never
> washed, rubbed with salt, and wrapped in cloth.
> No one had the slightest interest in you; no one
> pitied you or cared for you. On the day you were
> born, you were unwanted, dumped in a field and
> left to die. But I came by and saw you there, help-
> lessly kicking about in your own blood. As you
> lay there, I said, "Live!"
> —EZEKIEL 16:3–6

God begins by revealing both where Jerusalem was located and the genealogical origins of those who founded the city. He starts off by saying, "You are nothing but a Canaanite," implying that the land was already cursed. Why? Because Noah cursed Canaan (Gen. 9) when his father, Ham, saw Noah's nakedness and tried to expose him to his brother. Canaan was Ham's firstborn son and ultimately the recipient of a curse that would remain active up until the cross of Christ.

What does this mean? God was saying, "You were born cursed—from your very inception, there was already a curse applied through your great-great-great-great-great-grandfather Ham." We too are born in sin as the result of not just Adam's sin but also the personal sins of our ancestors. God gives a description of the maternal and paternal origins of the city of Jerusalem: from the father's side Amorite, and from the mother's side Hittite. Look at the Hebrew name meanings of each:

Canaanite: to be depressed (lowland peoples)[3]

Amorite: bitter; rebel; a babbler (highland peoples); hence "Babylon"[4]

Hittite: terror, terrible[5]

If we were to substitute the Hebrew name meanings and insert them into the verse we just read, this is how it would read. It's safe to say this is probably what God was saying:

> You were born depressed [Canaan] because your father was bitter [Amorite] and your mother was terrible [Hittite].

This would explain a lot as to why Jerusalem throughout the Old Testament and even today has been a troubled city. Many times in Scripture other nations are quoted as saying that Jerusalem is a trouble-maker city filled with violence. This is no different from most people who are born into the world: they are born into trouble!

God goes on to say to Jerusalem that the day you were founded as a city, no one *cut your umbilical cord*, implying the city still had a deep connection to its mother. Right here it's clear that the stronger hereditary sins were coming from the mother's side. Many of you can identify with this. Although both of your parents may have had issues, usually there is one side you carry the most hereditary sins from, as opposed to the other.

The verse continues, saying that no one took the time to cut your umbilical cord, implying that this needs to be done by someone who knows how to cut it—someone specialized in helping people cut ties to ungodly things. Helping people break ties who are still connected to the mother. This is a clear depiction of helping people break generational curses! If you're having a hard time seeing that in this verse, maybe it's because someone told you that generational curses do not exist for the believer.

God continues, saying that no one washed you. There is only one way you can be washed, and that is through the Word. (See Ephesians 5.) When a person is taken through deliverance and the generational curses are renounced and revoked, there has to be a declaration of Scripture to wash the person thoroughly from all the filth the curse caused in their life and also to establish some rules so they don't get cursed again.

In the Old Testament, God tried to do this through the Law of Moses and the prophets, but the people rejected them and even killed many of them. This is why Jesus wept over Jerusalem—because He was there to break their curses. But they refused and ultimately had Pontius Pilate crucify the One sent to cut their umbilical cord and wash them. This act of washing is needed because the baby is wallowing in blood, meaning there are bloodline issues. My heart is pounding as I type this because it's extremely clear that this metaphor fits the title of this book; the secret to generational curses is hidden in this text that God is revealing!

Rubbing salt on a newborn after cleaning off the blood is an ancient practice, though no longer practiced in Western civilization. It was done to ensure the child's skin would harden after washing. Salt is used to dry up water, and as it does, the skin hardens. During deliverance to break generational curses, we are helping someone to harden their resistance against opening the door to the iniquities they just got delivered from. If they don't, it's more than likely this person will revert to bondage. Just like the city of Jerusalem, God would send breakthrough after breakthrough, but they would eventually fall back into sin. Deliverance workers training to help people break curses must also help them become militant through Scripture to maintain their freedom and harden up against sin, the flesh, and the devil.

Finally, the newborn is wrapped in swaddling cloth. This is where we call on the Holy Spirit to fill all areas once dominated by demons and curses and saturate them with

His presence. Without this the newborn is uncovered and vulnerable to attack. The act of covering is the Holy Spirit's function once a person gets set free from a curse. An immediate supernatural manifestation of peace envelops the person. Now that they are cleaned up and free, they will be more sensitive to God's presence.

It wasn't until the day of Pentecost that Jerusalem received the baptism of the Holy Spirit, but again most of the people refused. In a deliverance session the Holy Spirit will cause the believer to surrender their mind, will, and emotions to Him, providing a spiritual covering and protection. First Peter says that what Israel and the prophets "wore" wasn't for themselves but for us.

> They were told that their messages were not for themselves, but for you. And now this Good News has been announced to you by those who preached in the power of the Holy Spirit sent from heaven. It is all so wonderful that even the angels are eagerly watching these things happen.
> —1 PETER 1:12

TREES, THE FAMILY TREE, AND FRUIT

All through the Gospels we've heard the proverb that a tree is known by its fruit. While this phrase means that a person's actions will identify who they really are, it also has a deeper meaning. In Scripture, trees have always been used symbolically to represent people, households, and bloodlines.

> And he shall be like a *tree* planted by the rivers of
> water, that bringeth forth his fruit in his season;
> his leaf also shall not wither; and whatsoever he
> doeth shall prosper.
>
> —Psalm 1:3, KJV

Other passages actually prove this point, especially the story of the blind man Jesus had to lay hands on twice. What the blind man said stands out: "I see men as trees." This is not written here for no reason, nor is this story trying to say that Jesus lacked the power to heal the man the first time that He laid hands on him. I believe it was purposely left in Scripture to further drive the revelation of men being trees and these trees bearing fruit.

> And he looked up, and said, I see men as *trees*,
> walking. After that he put his hands again upon
> his eyes, and made him look up: and he was
> restored, and saw every man clearly.
>
> —Mark 8:24–25, KJV

Not all trees (humans) give good fruit, and not all trees give bad fruit. But one thing we do know is that all trees give fruit. There is no way around it; what a person has in his heart will eventually be displayed by actions or expressed by the words spoken out of his mouth.

> For a good *tree* does not bear bad fruit, nor does a
> bad tree bear good fruit. For every *tree* is known
> by its own fruit. For men do not gather figs from
> thorns, nor do they gather grapes from a bram-
> ble bush. A good man out of the good treasure of

> his heart brings forth good; and an evil man out
> of the evil treasure of his heart brings forth evil.
> For out of the abundance of the heart his mouth
> speaks.
>
> —Luke 6:43–45, NKJV

You're probably saying to yourself, Pagani is stretching the text right now in saying people are "trees" in Scripture. Honestly, I'm not. In the Book of Daniel we find Nebuchadnezzar having a dream that causes him to call all his magicians to inquire of its interpretation. None of his magicians are able to interpret or reveal the dream, not even under threat of death, so Daniel is summoned and given the task of revealing the dream and interpreting it. Nebuchadnezzar tells Daniel,

> While I was lying in my bed, this is what I
> dreamed. I saw a large tree in the middle of the
> earth. The tree grew very tall and strong, reaching high into the heavens for all the world to see.
>
> —Daniel 4:10–11

Daniel in turn tells the king that the tree is Nebuchadnezzar himself and his current role as the emperor of Babylon.

> That *tree*, Your Majesty, is you. For you have
> grown strong and great; your greatness reaches
> up to heaven, and your rule to the ends of the
> earth.
>
> —Daniel 4:22

So as you can see, all human beings are "trees" in the garden of God. Understanding this will help make sense of the concept of a family tree or why we even use that term. Numerous verses of Scripture help to solidify this point of people as trees. Without making this revelation of the tree a doctrine (because it's not), now every time you read in Scripture where the text speaks of trees you can safely look at it symbolically—not all the time, but sometimes (the Holy Spirit will show you)—and make the correlation to people, households, or bloodlines. Which leads us to Aaron's rod blossoming.

During the Israelites' journey in the wilderness, a man named Korah—a relative of Moses and Aaron—decided to lead an insurrection against Moses, Aaron, and Miriam. This group of about 250 persons began to poison the minds of other members of the tribe of Levi, saying that Moses and Aaron weren't the only ones who could hear from God. The Lord heard their rebellion and called for a meeting with all the leaders of the tribes. He commanded them to bring their staffs and place them before the tabernacle, and He said whosoever's staff began to sprout, that would be the man God had chosen.

> Then the LORD said to Moses, "Tell the people of Israel to bring you twelve wooden staffs, one from each leader of Israel's ancestral tribes, and inscribe each leader's name on his staff. Inscribe Aaron's name on the staff of the tribe of Levi, for there must be one staff for the leader of each ancestral tribe. Place these staffs in the

> Tabernacle in front of the Ark containing the
> tablets of the Covenant, where I meet with you.
> Buds will sprout on the staff belonging to the
> man I choose. Then I will finally put an end to
> the people's murmuring and complaining against
> you."
>
> —NUMBERS 17:1–5

The following day, when Moses and Aaron and the elders of Israel returned to the Tabernacle, they found that Aaron's staff, representing the tribe of Levi, had sprouted, budded, blossomed, and produced ripe almonds (v. 8). Why would God require a staff to be brought to the tabernacle? Because a staff is a piece of wood that is cut from a tree. A staff is really a large branch, and it represents particular households from a family tree. Even Jesus in Scripture is called "the Branch"—but I will leave that revelation for another day.

God made clear that Aaron's family was selected to serve as high priest because of the almonds that sprouted. God wants to cause your staff to sprout. It's His desire to bless not just you but also your family bloodline. All families of the earth are trees before Him, and each particular family, if they honor God, can have the blessing of the Lord's name over their bloodline or decree a blessing over their bloodline. Look at the following verse:

> So I cared for the flock intended for slaughter—
> the flock that was oppressed. Then I took two
> shepherd's staffs and named one Favor and the
> other Union.
>
> —ZECHARIAH 11:7

God actually took two staffs to represent particular families of the children of Israel and called one *favor* and the other *union*—meaning that these households would experience the favor of God all their days. If you're reading this, I want you to claim that for your family. Claim that God's favor would be upon you and your bloodline and that you would all serve God. You don't have to settle for just being saved and going through the motions; you can have life, and life more abundantly. If heaven can decree *favor* over a staff, heaven also wants to decree *healing*, wants to decree *breakthrough*, wants to decree *excellence* (or honor) over you. God also decreed that there would be a *union*. The text doesn't say exactly what that union would consist of, but we can speculate that there were things heaven was going to unite with them.

Without getting all preachy, I want God to bring me into *union* with the right people, with the right relationships, with the right choices, with the right decisions. I want my life to be in union with the Holy Spirit and the Word of God so that everything I do pleases Him. But there is a flip side to that: when a family that started out honoring God in everything they do abandons the law of God and reverts to living in sin, well, that same measure of favor gets cut off, and God does the opposite.

> Then I took my staff called Favor and cut it in two, showing that I had revoked the covenant I had made with all the nations. That was the end of my covenant with them. The suffering flock was

watching me, and they knew that the LORD was
speaking through my actions [favor cut in two].
—ZECHARIAH 11:10–11

Right now ask the Lord to cause your staff—your life
and family—to be blessed and sprout so that all your
branches—your descendants—can be under the blessing of
the Lord.

PRAYER OF FAMILY BLESSING

*God of Abraham, Isaac, and Jacob, I'm asking
that You would cause Your favor and union to
fall upon me and my family. I'm asking You to
help us to honor You in everything that we do.*

CONCLUDING THOUGHTS

As we close this chapter, we've only scratched the surface of
what heaven is going to show you. Get yourself a pad and
pen to write down what the Holy Spirit will reveal to you
as you continue to read this book. You will be challenged,
you will be confronted, but you will heal, and you will also
be set free. Get ready because there is a lot more to go. May
the righteous Judge give you strength as your trial of being
set free begins!

CHAPTER 3

THE CURSE AND THE COURTROOM

So I confronted them and *called down curses* on them. I beat some of them and pulled out their hair. I made them swear in the name of God that they would not let their children intermarry with the pagan people of the land.

—NEHEMIAH 13:25

Like a flitting sparrow, like a flying swallow, so a curse *without cause* shall not alight.

—PROVERBS 26:2, NKJV

However, if you do not obey the LORD your God and do not carefully follow all his commands and decrees I am giving you today, all these *curses will come* on you and overtake you.

—DEUTERONOMY 28:15, NIV

C URSES DID NOT have their origin on earth but rather in heaven. When Lucifer sinned against the Lord, the Bible says that iniquity was first found in Lucifer and later began to transfer onto anyone who followed in his footsteps.

Thou wast perfect in thy ways from the day that thou wast created, till iniquity was found in thee.

—EZEKIEL 28:15, KJV

The Book of Hebrews says that one of Jesus' roles after the resurrection and ascension was to purify the heavens, meaning that Lucifer's sin had contaminated everything and caused the curse of the Lord to transfer onto everything he touched (Heb. 9:22).

When man sinned, the curse of the Lord was already in existence in the universe, and Satan was looking to transfer it upon God's newest creation—and he succeeded. This is the main reason why Satan, demons, and fallen angels who followed after Satan have no forgiveness but remain perpetually under the curse of the Lord.

GENERATIONAL CURSES IN THE BLOODLINE

Generational curses in the bloodline is a real thing. And the following scriptures describe it the best. During the children of Israel's journey in the desert, one day a half-Israelite man got into a fight with a fellow Jew, and during the fight he blasphemed the name of the Lord with a curse.

> One day a man who had an Israelite mother and an Egyptian father came out of his tent and got into a fight with one of the Israelite men. During the fight, this son of an Israelite woman blasphemed the Name of the LORD with a curse.
> —LEVITICUS 24:10–11

One of the Ten Commandments was "thou shalt not take the name of the LORD thy God in vain" (Exod. 20:7, KJV). This was a serious infraction that had a penalty of death attached to it. What is interesting about this young man is that he wasn't a full-blooded Israelite; he was half Egyptian. This alone was already wrong in the eyes of the Lord, as Israel was forbidden by God to marry outside the nation. We don't have the history of how this man's mother connected with his father, but I'm sure it was during her stay in Egypt. And it's safe to say that his father didn't leave Egypt when the noted nation of Israel left with Moses. The text actually gives us this woman's name and her tribe:

> So the man was brought to Moses for judgment. His mother was Shelomith, the daughter of Dibri of the tribe of Dan.
>
> —LEVITICUS 24:11

The question has to be asked: Why did this man blaspheme the Lord with a curse in the middle of the fight when every Jew knew it was a death sentence? Well, it was because the Egyptian side of the family had a hatred for God.

> And they set on for him by himself, and for them by themselves, and for the Egyptians, which did eat with him, by themselves: because the Egyptians might not eat bread with the Hebrews; for that is an abomination unto the Egyptians.
>
> —GENESIS 43:32, KJV

A long history of hatred existed between the Egyptians and the Israelites. Hidden deep within the bloodline of every Egyptian was a disdain toward Israel that has carried from generation to generation. So when this Isra-elite man got into a fight with a fellow Jew, that curse of hatred reared its ugly head, and the demons attached to the curse directed their blasphemies toward heaven. I'm sure this man was surprised at what came out of his mouth, knowing what the penalty would be. This is exactly how generational curses operate. They remain in the bloodline, waiting for the right conditions to be met so they can man-ifest and take effect.

I've dealt with countless believers who love the Lord—many of whom serve in ministry—who for the most part are doing well, then out of nowhere this dark issue arises in their life, and they are left traumatized and discouraged as they battle sins and issues they didn't know existed in their life, or issues they see their parents or family strug-gling with. It rattles their theology because the Christian church doesn't teach on generational curses. So we are left to assume it's some emotional or mental thing that can be corrected with behavior modification, counseling, or ther-apy. (Please know I'm not opposed to those things; they should be pursued when needed.) But when it comes to generational curses, they can't be counseled out but rather must be renounced and cast out.

When a generational curse manifests, the first thing it does to the believer is place them in custody. Being in custody is not the same as being locked up through sen-tencing. I was sentenced to nine years in prison, and trust me when I tell you I would rather be in custody than in chains. Custody means you are in jail awaiting trial. You haven't been sentenced, so there is some freedom. You can move around—your freedom is only partially taken. When you're sentenced, your freedom is completely taken from you! Generational curses put Christians only partially in bondage, not completely. Most believers suffering from a generational curse can function normally and live for God, but there is one area they know they haven't been able to overcome, so like the man in the following verse, they have to "sit in jail" and wait for their case to be brought up in the heavenly council.

> They kept the man in custody until the LORD's will in the matter should become clear to them.
> —LEVITICUS 24:12

Unfortunately for this man, when the time came for his case to be seen by God, the punishment was death. And those who heard the curse were to lay hands on his head and transfer the curse back before they were spiritually contaminated. All generational curses not resolved will eventually cause great heartache and pain mentally, spiritually, and emotionally. Jesus wants to set you free from the hidden curses in your bloodline that are waiting for just the right time to come out. Finish reading the story.

> Then the LORD said to Moses, "Take the blasphemer outside the camp, and tell all those who heard the curse to lay their hands on his head. Then let the entire community stone him to death. Say to the people of Israel: Those who curse their God will be punished for their sin. Anyone who blasphemes the Name of the LORD

> must be stoned to death by the whole commu-
> nity of Israel. Any native-born Israelite or for-
> eigner among you who blasphemes the Name of
> the LORD must be put to death."
>
> —LEVITICUS 24:13–16

The great news is that unlike the man in this story, you're not without hope. Jesus came to set the captives free, and He took upon Himself the curse of the law so that you can be made the righteousness of God in Him. The Holy Spirit has been given to you as a helper, and He will keep you from making any mistakes in this walk that would trigger a generational curse. That makes for great rejoicing—to know that the Holy Spirit will keep you from falling and present you as a spotless bride ready to meet the Bridegroom.

THE COURTROOM OF HEAVEN

Deliverance from generational curses is not a religious experience, it's a legal exchange. Why? Everything in existence is maintained and controlled by the courtroom of heaven, and that courtroom is within the kingdom. Jesus said in His model prayer, "Thy kingdom come, Thy will be done in earth, as it is in heaven" (Matt. 6:9–13, KJV).

What is the kingdom? In his book *Kingdom Principles*, the late Dr. Myles Munroe defined the kingdom as "the sovereign rule of a king over territory (domain), impacting it with his will, purpose, and intent."[1] In this biblical text Jesus uses the word *kingdom* to refer to God's government, rulership, and dominion over the earth. The kingdom of God encompasses God's will executed, God's jurisdiction, heaven's influence, God's administration, and God's impact and influence. With this foundational understanding, everything you read in this book will make a lot more sense—and I'm hoping it will spark inspiration for you to see things legally and not relationally. Without this view, *The Secrets to Generational Curses* is nothing more than speculation and eisegesis! But it's not. We are reading a legal document.

Within the kingdom of God there is a courtroom, and this courtroom establishes the constitution and laws by which this kingdom is governed. The Bible is our "constitution." This kingdom also has an army that is equipped to protect the kingdom from being assaulted. What I am trying to establish is that everything is legal! Even the word *testament* is a legal word. It means "will." Both the Old and New Testaments are legal documents. When we quote Scripture, we are quoting the laws of the constitution of the kingdom of heaven. When a person or demon violates any of these laws, there are penalties to pay.

> Then Micaiah continued, "Listen to what the
> LORD says! I saw the LORD sitting on his throne
> with all the armies of heaven around him, on
> his right and on his left. And the LORD said,
> 'Who can entice Ahab to go into battle against
> Ramoth-gilead so he can be killed?' There were
> many suggestions, and finally a spirit approached
> the LORD and said, 'I can do it!' 'How will you
> do this?' the LORD asked. And the spirit replied,
> 'I will go out and inspire all of Ahab's prophets to

speak lies.' 'You will succeed,' said the LORD. 'Go ahead and do it.' So you see, the LORD has put a lying spirit in the mouths of all your prophets. For the LORD has pronounced your doom."

—1 KINGS 22:19–23

We also find in the Book of Job a court deliberation between Satan the accuser and the Lord (the righteous Judge) concerning Job. This was being held in the courtroom of heaven—and we all know the outcome. I'm hoping that at this point your paradigm is shifting to think about biblical things more legally.

VENGEANCE VS. REVENGE

It's never personal but all legal. Our God is righteous and fair; this needs to be established because it's one thing to have a perfect legal system, but it's another to have a perverted judge abusing that system. (This is why many times in the Bible, God condemned judges who took bribes.) All judges on the earth are an extension of God, so when a judge is perverted and doesn't deal in righteousness, justice is perverted.

The LORD demands accurate scales and balances; he sets the standards for fairness.

—PROVERBS 16:11

The LORD detests double standards; he is not pleased by dishonest scales.

—PROVERBS 20:23

Since the Judge of all creation is just, then all His judgments are based in fairness. This is why if a generational curse is active in someone's life and bloodline, someone did something to cause it. If the Judge is forced to act because of a curse, just know it's not personal but legal! Justice carried out that is personal is not justice but revenge. There is a difference between revenge and vengeance. Revenge is the action of *inflicting* hurt or harm on someone for an injury or wrong suffered at their hands. But vengeance is punishment *inflicted* or retribution *exacted* for an injury or wrong. *They are not the same thing.* God never takes revenge; He always exacts vengeance.

> Dearly beloved, avenge not yourselves, but rather give place unto wrath: for it is written, Vengeance is mine; I will repay, saith the Lord.
> —ROMANS 12:19, KJV

Let's go further into understanding how vengeance and generational curses work together.

THE LORD TAKES VENGEANCE

During the time of King Ahab, one day he saw a vineyard he really liked that belonged to Naboth. The king offered him a large sum of money to buy it, but Naboth refused because it was his only vineyard and part of his family inheritance. The king returned to the palace saddened by the decline, and his wife, Jezebel, heard of it and devised a plan to have Naboth killed and his vineyard given to the king. On the surface it looked like a normal transfer of property, but the means by which it was done was evil. Jezebel invited Naboth as an honored guest, then hired false accusers to stand up in the middle of dinner and accuse him of blasphemy. Naboth was stoned to death, and his property was given to the king—but heaven saw this evil plot and judged the bloodline of Ahab for it.

> You are to destroy the family of Ahab; you will avenge the murder of my prophets and of all my other people who were killed by Jezebel. The entire family of Ahab must be wiped out—every male, no matter who. I will destroy the family of Ahab as I destroyed the families of Jeroboam (son of Nebat) and of Baasha (son of Ahijah). Dogs shall eat Ahab's wife Jezebel at Jezreel, and no one will bury her.
>
> —2 KINGS 9:7–10, TLB

> "I will repay him here on Naboth's property for the murder of Naboth and his sons." So throw him out on Naboth's field, just as the Lord said.
>
> —2 KINGS 9:26, TLB

In this matter, the Lord didn't take revenge. I'm sure Naboth's family desired revenge. But instead God decided to take vengeance. Many generational curses are nothing more than heaven taking vengeance for crimes—physical and spiritual—done by our ancestors.

LAWS OF THE COURTROOM

The following list, in my opinion, will be the most important segment you read in this book, as it describes the different categories of legal terms all through Scripture that the average churchgoer and Bible reader has glanced over as they read the Word. If you look closely at the next verse, you will see that there is a distinction in these different categories.

> Thou camest down also upon mount Sinai, and spakest with them from heaven, and gavest them right *judgments*, and true *laws*, good *statutes* and *commandments*: and madest known unto them thy holy sabbath, and commandedst them *precepts*, statutes, and laws, by the hand of Moses thy servant.
>
> —NEHEMIAH 9:13–14, KJV

Just as different legal terms produce different results in a courtroom, the same is true with the kingdom of God. Knowing these terms will allow the believer to know how to approach God and get the results they're looking for in Christ!

> The law of the LORD is perfect, converting the soul: the testimony of the LORD is sure, making wise the simple. The statutes of the LORD are right, rejoicing the heart: the commandment of the LORD is pure, enlightening the eyes. The fear of the LORD is clean, enduring for ever: the

> judgments of the LORD are true and righteous
> altogether.
>
> —PSALM 19:7–9, KJV

Here are the different legal categories connected to the courtroom of heaven. You will find these terms all through Scripture.

Decree (Lev. 26:46)—"a formal and authoritative order, especially one having the force of law; a judicial decision or order; to command, ordain, or decide by decree."[2]

Law (Neh. 9:13, KJV)—the Hebrew word *torah* means teaching and direction for life and is the word most often used for the laws and principles Yahweh has given to His people for their benefit and spiritual well-being.[3]

Statute (Neh. 9:13, KJV)—"a law enacted by the legislative branch of a government; an act of a corporation or of its founder intended as a *permanent* rule."[4] *Statute* comes from the Latin root word meaning "to stand"; whereas a *statue* (which shares the same root word) literally stands, often on two legs, a *statute* is a law that stands.[5]

Regulation (Lev. 26:46)—"an official rule that controls the way that things are done; control of an activity, process, or industry by official rules."[6] Such regulations aren't sin if not obeyed.

Commandment (Neh. 9:13, NKJV)—in its primary meaning, the Hebrew word *mitzvah* is "an expression of the will of God" and includes "not only an 'order' to do something, but also the moral imperative or obligation to do it."[7] The word *command* implies force or power, as a general commands his troops. To disobey a commandment would be an act of insubordination.

Judgment (Neh. 9:13, KJV)—denotes the process whereby a verdict is reached, or the verdict itself; a judgment is bound up with the notions of justice, meaning the righteous way of doing something. The Free (Legal) Dictionary defines judgment as "a decision by a court or other tribunal that resolves a controversy and determines the rights and obligations of the parties."[8]

Testimony (Ps. 93:5, KJV)—the Hebrew word *eduth* refers to a witness or testimony but is normally used in terms of legally binding stipulations or laws. This word refers to that witness which confirms the truth to be so; a testimony in a court of law.[9] (These are testimonies sent by God Himself to verify a truth or commandment, e.g., Aaron's staff, the jar full of manna, etc.)

Precept (Neh. 9:14, KJV)—"a rule or direction, often with some religious basis, dictating a way you should act or behave."[10]

TEMPORARY LAWS (CONCESSIONS)

Concessions are temporary laws established to regulate bad behavior. Once the behavior has been modified by the guilty person(s), the law is changed and removed.

> But I am saying this as a concession, not as a command.
>
> —1 CORINTHIANS 7:6, AMP

Concession—"an act or instance of conceding, granting, or yielding. A thing conceded or granted; acknowledgment, as of an argument or claim."[11]

In 1 Corinthians 14 we find Paul giving a concession that women are to be "silent in the church" (v. 34), and if they have any questions they're to ask their husbands at home. This concession was given because during the time of the birthing of the Corinthian church some women were being nosey and interrupting their husbands in the middle of the preaching. So Paul established this concession to help the women regulate this behavior. *It was not meant to be a perpetual law!* Paul didn't want women never to speak in the church for all ages to come; rather he wanted the women of Corinth to be more self-controlled in their behavior as concerning order in the Christian church, which was new to them.

Please note that not all concessions are meant to be permanent!

Almost two thousand years later we have many mainline denominations prohibiting women from teaching, preaching, and being ordained into the ministry.

Another example of a concession is the bill of divorce. It's very interesting that we find Jesus saying the bill of divorce was only allowed by Moses because of the hardness of people's hearts. This is why Jesus had to address the issue during His Sermon on the Mount three thousand years later.

> "Well, he permitted it," they replied. "He said a man can give his wife a written notice of divorce and send her away." But Jesus responded, "He

wrote this commandment only as a concession to
your hard hearts."

—MARK 10:4–5

Now let's finally begin to address curses and generational curses and how to deal with them.

WHAT IS A CURSE?

In Hebrew, the word for *curse* is *arur*, which carries "a sense
of *divinely imposed* bad luck or misfortune," or rather the
unfortunate circumstance that befalls a person as a result
of the Lord directly sending it your way.[12] What does this
mean? It means that a curse *is not a demon!* Demons carry
out the curse imposed by the courtroom of heaven, but they
are not the initiators of it. If this distinction isn't made, we
will wrongly credit the devil for what irresponsible sinful
behavior initiated.

What is a biblical curse in a legal sense? A curse is a warranted verdict given by the courtroom of heaven against a
person, household, or place that committed a transgression
against God's law. Not every sin warrants a curse, but there
are some that will. A curse is a divinely imposed judgment
that causes misfortune in someone's life.

DEMONS AND THE CURSE

Demons are enforcers of the curse, not the initiators of
it. Demons can't impose a curse on someone unless they
have a legal right to do so. They carry out the judgment
that the courtroom of heaven has sanctioned. To help you

understand, demons carrying out a curse are like US Marshals removing a squatter who has failed to pay his or her rent or mortgage. They've been given authority to carry out the judgment given by the court. The kingdom of darkness is the same. We see this in the life of Job. Before all the calamity that happened to him, we find a court proceeding in motion where Satan asks permission to attack Job. The Lord grants that permission, and Satan goes and carries out the judgment.

> "All right, you may test him," the LORD said to Satan. "Do whatever you want with everything he possesses, but don't harm him physically." So Satan left the LORD's presence.
>
> —JOB 1:12

Satan was given authority to carry out the curse and cause misfortune to hit everything Job owned, including his physical health—but the curse had a restriction: "Do not harm him physically." This is exactly what demons do when carrying out a curse. They can only go as far as the judgment of the curse permits. Anything further than that would be unjust. The courtroom of heaven is dictating everything, stipulating and controlling everything!

To help you further understand, we see this in the life of King Saul, when he eventually lost favor with God through his many acts of rebellion, and the courtroom of heaven cursed him. God told Samuel to no longer pray for Saul, because heaven had rejected him.

> Now the LORD said to Samuel, "You have mourned long enough for Saul. I have rejected him as king of Israel."
>
> —1 SAMUEL 16:1

Immediately after that judgment, the Bible says a tormenting spirit "*from* God" began to afflict Saul (v. 15). For years I never understood what "from God" meant. My evangelical mindset at that time (I was a new believer) just couldn't see a loving God sending a demon on someone, but when you look at the events of Saul's life from a legal perspective, it's easy to understand.

> But one day when Saul was sitting at home, with spear in hand, the tormenting spirit from the LORD suddenly came upon him again. As David played his harp.
>
> —1 SAMUEL 19:9

God found Saul guilty of rebellion and judged him. The verdict was that the presence of the Lord would no longer be on him and heaven would no longer talk to him through prayer. This verdict was immediately given to the kingdom of darkness, and the demons were dispatched to attack him.

The biblical passages of the courtroom of heaven cursing someone and demons carrying out those curses, or verdicts, are numerous, from King Ahab to Gehazi (Elisha's servant) to Judas Iscariot.

What Is a Generational Curse?

A generational curse is a warranted verdict given by the courtroom of heaven against a household that committed a transgression against God's law. It's basically the same as a curse, but instead of a person it's against a family unit. The only difference is that when God is cursing a household, the judgment keeps transferring down the bloodline until the demands of justice have been satisfied. The text says this happens unto the third and fourth generation.

> You shall not bow down to any images nor worship them in any way, for I am the Lord your God. I am a jealous God, and I will bring *the curse* of a father's sins upon even the third and fourth generation of the children of those who hate me; but I will show kindness to a thousand generations of those who love me and keep my commandments.
> —Deuteronomy 5:9–10, TLB

We can see examples of generational curses in everyday life when we witness celebrities or influential families who seem to have this strange misfortune that spreads to almost all family members—so much so that people start saying "the curse of _____ [family last name]."

Analogy of a Rape Case

Let me further explain how a generational curse works by giving you an analogy of a rape case.

Scripture has a different view than American

evangelicalism as to why God sets you free. God doesn't set you free because He loves you (even though He does love you); He sets you free because the demands of justice have been satisfied, and the demands of justice being satisfied is because *He loves you*! Now why am I saying this? Here's the analogy.

Let's say as a Christian your only daughter was raped. (God forbid, but for the sake of this analogy, let me finish.) Would you want your daughter's rapist to be caught? Any good parent would want this person caught and brought to justice. Why? Because your love for your daughter requires it. Any parent who sincerely loves their daughter would want justice. Does God want justice? Of course He does. Why? Because His justice *demands* it. How long would you pursue your daughter's rapist? If you're honest, the answer is until this person is caught! Why? Because love never fails, and it will require justice until the man is apprehended. How long will God's justice pursue this person? Well, until the demands of justice have been satisfied!

Let's say that the rapist is never caught during your lifetime, and you die. Would you still require justice for your daughter from beyond the grave? Of course, because your love for your daughter is now everlasting. Does God still demand justice for your daughter even though you're dead? Of course, because God never dies. He will continue to pursue the rapist until he is caught.

Now why does God continue this pursuit? Because God is *love* and God is *just*! God knows exactly where the rapist is and has been at work behind the scenes—and will continue to do so—until the demands of His justice have been satisfied. Rape is a serious sin in the courtroom of heaven, and its penalties are severe. God won't stop!

Let's say heaven finally has the rapist cornered and is about to enact judgment for what he did to your daughter many years earlier, and at that moment he repents for his sins and asks Christ to be his Savior. What happens to the rapist? Does God overlook his rape? If He does, then His love for you as a believer is in question because God promised you justice. Should the rapist be forgiven? Of course. Why? Because the penalty for his sins has been paid by Christ's work on the cross. The penalty of death for the sin of rape has been satisfied. He will enjoy spending eternity with Jesus.

The question I have is, Does the story of the rapist end with him getting away with rape simply because he became a Christian? I know we've been trained to say yes, but truthfully the answer is no. Though the rapist will not suffer eternal death, the demands of justice haven't been fully satisfied. Why? Not all court cases that end with a guilty verdict are sentenced only to prison time. Sometimes there are other penalties the person has to pay included with their prison sentence. Some are required to pay certain amounts of money. The same is true with generational curses. The believer is forgiven upon repenting of his sins and believing in the finished work of Christ on the cross, but other penalties required by the courtroom of heaven have to be sorted out through the Christian experience until the demands of justice are fully satisfied. Generational curses aren't a salvation issue but rather a "paying other penalties" issue.

Now let's get into six ways in which you can become cursed.

CHAPTER 4

SIX PRIMARY WAYS CURSES HAPPEN

THE BIBLE IS very clear that a curse doesn't come without a cause (Prov. 26:2), so the primary way a curse is activated is by someone initiating it.

1. CURSED THROUGH ACTIONS

Heaven isn't going around cursing people at random; someone has to initiate the curse. Humans curse themselves either by ignorance or by violating, ignoring, and rejecting God's laws. Adam didn't curse himself by mistake; he willfully made the choice to eat from the tree of the knowledge of good and evil. When he did, he opened the door to disobedience, and the curse was activated.

As a matter of fact, the first time we ever see the word *curse* is found in Genesis 3 with God cursing the serpent, then cursing Eve for eating the fruit and causing her husband to eat, and then cursing Adam for allowing himself to be influenced by Eve and eating too. God is just. He doesn't curse anyone who doesn't deserve it. Pray this prayer of freedom, and break the curse that was activated by your actions.

PRAYER OF FREEDOM

Heavenly Father, I come before Your courtroom to ask for Your forgiveness. I repent for opening the door to sin and activating the curse in my life and bloodline. I plead with You to break the generational curse and start afresh with me and my bloodline now, in Jesus' name!

2. CURSED THROUGH PARTNERSHIP (PHARAOH)

The second way you can become cursed is through your partnership with someone who is cursed, and the consequences of that curse transfer onto everyone who is in partnership with that person. We see in Genesis 12 that the whole land of Egypt was placed under a curse of barrenness because Pharaoh took Sarai into his harem, unaware that she was Abram's wife. The Lord closed the wombs of all Egyptian women as the result of Pharaoh's actions. *Innocence is not an excuse.* Though Pharaoh was innocent in this instance, heaven still activated a curse. It wasn't until Pharaoh returned Sarai to Abram that the curse was lifted. It does matter who you partner with, especially in relationships, business, church covering, and living quarters. As believers we need to pray about everything, especially in matters of whom we connect with. Here is a prayer of freedom to help you get set free from curses of partnership.

PRAYER OF FREEDOM

Lord Jesus, forgive my partnership with others who are cursed by You. You warned us in Scripture not to be unequally yoked together with unbelievers. I repent for this partnership and ask that You would sever it in the spirit and cause all curses to be revoked, in Jesus' name!

3. CURSED THROUGH WORDS

The worlds that we see, both physical and spiritual, were formed by one thing—words! Hebrews 11:3 says, "By faith we understand that the entire universe was formed at God's command." The same can be said about the "universe" we are raised in and who we are to become as people. If we're raised in a loving environment with words that are nurturing, affirming, and corrective, we will grow up emotionally and mentally stable people who can function as God intended in our families. But if we're raised in an environment where words of belittlement and rejection are the norm, then the curses attached to those words will be activated. The Bible says "death and life are in the power of the tongue" (Prov. 18:21, KJV), which means our tongues do have the power to set off a chain of events that brings either life to a person or death.

When a child is constantly told they are "good for nothing" in the early years of their life by their parents or guardians, the curse of worthlessness or lack of self-worth is activated. If these curses aren't confronted and renounced, the child will grow up with these active curses in their life and transfer them to their children. Most of us can recollect memories of families we know (or even our own families) where the majority of the family members grew up dealing with the same lack of verbal affirmation and rejection, and their lives did not reach the fullest potential that God intended.

For many of you reading this right now, the Holy Spirit is revealing that word curses have been affecting you since you were _____ (name the age the Holy Spirit reveals to you). Pray the following prayer, and break these curses off your life.

PRAYER OF FREEDOM

Lord God, I repent for all words spoken out of my mouth that cause deep hurt to others, to myself, and to Your kingdom. Forgive me, Lord. May all negative words spoken over my life also be broken. May every generational curse be broken now, in Jesus' name!

4. CURSED THROUGH ITEMS (ACHAN'S BABYLONIAN TUNIC)

The next way a believer can be cursed, and probably the most ignorant, is by bringing accursed items into their home. Leviticus strongly warns the children of Israel not to bring any accursed things into their homes. What is an accursed thing? The Bible uses the word *anathema*, meaning "devoted to destruction," letting us know that such items have been deemed by heaven as something to be thrown away.[1] When a believer ignorantly or knowingly brings such items into their home, the Scriptures say that their home also becomes devoted to destruction.

I remember many years ago when the Harry Potter movies came out and many Christians were going against them. I decided to buy the *Harry Potter and the Chamber of Secrets* DVD to investigate if the claims were true or just a bunch of Christians being fanatical. Later that night my youngest son, Xavier, who was around seven years old, started screaming that there were spiders all over his stomach. When I went to search him, there was nothing there, so I assured him there were no spiders. About an hour later he screamed again, saying there were spiders on his stomach. I looked, and there was nothing, but I was upset for being awakened in the night, as I had to go to work the next morning. So I told him sternly to go to bed.

Thirty minutes later he got up screaming, saying the same thing—but this time a thought crossed my mind that maybe my son was being attacked by demons. So I prayed and asked the Lord, and He reminded me that I had the Harry Potter DVD on my dresser, which I never watched. I asked God to forgive me, then broke the DVD and threw it out my window. (Yes, littering is wrong, but I was desperate.) My son went back to sleep and stayed asleep for the rest of the night.

Years later, when one of the Harry Potter movies was shown on television, I sensed something telling me to watch it. So while I was cleaning my home, I watched the movie, and about halfway through there is a scene where Harry Potter needs to obtain information from an evil creature deep in the woods. Upon arriving, the creature is revealed to be one *big spider* with millions of smaller spiders surrounding it, trying to eat him. Right then I knew bringing that DVD into my home years earlier had opened a door to the demons attached to the movie itself.

My inbox has been flooded with hundreds of emails throughout the years from Christians experiencing the same thing when bringing various items into their homes. A classic biblical example of this is found in Joshua 7, when Achan takes a Babylonian tunic and hides it among his own stuff. This one act of disobedience causes the children of Israel to lose one of their first major battles when entering the Promised Land.

When Joshua and the elders inquire of the Lord as to why they lost the battle, the Lord's reply is, "Israel has sinned….They have even taken some of the accursed things, and…put it among their own stuff" (v. 11, NKJV). Through the casting of lots they discover that Achan is the transgressor. The consequence is the death penalty for both him and his family. Why his family? Because a tunic of high value could be transferred from Achan to his children upon his death and thereby spread the curse from one generation to the next.

Heaven's response to such items is to *get rid of them*! Without getting too superstitious or fanatical, we also need to be careful with various gifts we received of which we don't know the origin. When we travel and purchase figurines, buy jewelry from other countries, and so forth, we need to be sensitive to any warnings from the Holy Spirit. Sometimes items of sentimental value given to us by those we love can have their origins in witchcraft. The children of Israel were told that having such accursed items among their possessions would bring nothing but 100 percent defeat.

God's remedy to resolve this curse? Get rid of the accursed items!

The text is clear that God told Joshua to get rid of the accursed thing, and once done, His favor would again rest on the children of Israel in their conquest of the land of Canaan. Right now, pray the following prayer and ask the Holy Spirit to reveal to you what you may have in your possession that could bring dishonor to God or give the enemy a foothold.

PRAYER OF FREEDOM

Holy Spirit, I ask for Your forgiveness for having items in my possession that are cursed by You. I repent for my ignorance in this matter. Please sever all demonic strongholds and curses that may have been activated in this area. Lord, send Your angels to clean my home of anything that opened the door to darkness! As for me and my house, we will serve the Lord. In Jesus' name, I pray.

Ask the Holy Spirit to reveal items in your home that may be causing a generational curse, and get rid of them.

You can list them here, then repent of these items, throw them away, and verbally command all demons to leave.

1. _____

2. _____

3. _____

4. _____

5. _____

6. _____

5. DISHONOR OF DIGNITARIES (GUARDIANS)

One sure way to become cursed or activate a curse is to slander and dishonor a dignitary. A dignitary is a person considered to be important because of high rank or office. In this sense I'm referring to either a parent(s), legal guardian(s), or someone of high authority in your life, such as a pastor or church leader. I'm aware that this particular curse hasn't been stressed enough, so what I'm saying might actually be new to many of you, but it's been in our face since the giving of the Law on Mount Sinai. It's found in the fifth commandment, which tells us to honor our fathers and mothers. If you look closely, you will see that it is the only commandment with a promise attached to it—but a curse is also implied there.

> Honor your father and mother. Then you will live a long, full life in the land the LORD your God is giving you.
>
> —EXODUS 20:12

The curse of premature death is attached to those *who don't* honor their father and mother. In the Old Testament we are commanded to honor the leaders of Israel.

> Do not blaspheme God or curse the ruler of your people.
>
> —EXODUS 22:28, NIV

Again we see that heaven is serious about us submitting to those in authority (parents and guardians) or those over us spiritually in the Lord. Scripture declares, "For rebellion is as the sin of witchcraft" (1 Sam. 15:23, NKJV). The offense of dishonoring those over you is so severe that heaven made it a commandment and exclusively attached a stipulation to those who follow it.

Through the years I've seen many believers who don't understand this principle go on to dishonor not just their parents but also their spiritual leaders (pastors) and face dire consequences. I'm not one to subscribe to the abuse of "touch not my anointed" in the church, but I do believe God's Word holds true in defending and upholding those who have been placed over us. To go even further, Romans

13 says we are to pray for those in authority over us (law enforcement officers, government officials, etc.) and submit to their rule so we can live peaceable lives. The consequence of not doing so is to bear judgment, "For he is God's minister to you for good...[and] does not bear the sword in vain" (v. 4, NKJV).

A lot of Christians have renounced all the other ways to get cursed but have been guilty of breaking this commandment and still find no breakthrough in their lives. They've fasted, prayed, and renounced, and yet they are still in defeat. Dishonor to dignitaries is the answer. Many times such dishonor is not done intentionally. Many years ago when I first opened our church, I invited a particular man of God to be a guest speaker for our church anniversary. The service went so well that I invited him a second time. After the preaching I gave him the lowest honorarium without considering that he drove six hours to get to our church. He never complained; he just took the honorarium and left.

Years later, out of nowhere, the Lord reminded me of that day and told me to find him and bless him with a $1,000 offering and ask for his forgiveness. I hadn't spoken to him since he visited our church many years earlier. When we talked on the phone, he had actually forgotten the incident, but I reminded him of how I unintentionally dishonored him and wanted to make it right. I sent him the financial gift, and while I was still talking to him, the notification bell on my phone dinged and someone randomly gave me $2,000. I had broken a particular curse of lack due to my negligence. I wonder how many curses believers have unintentionally activated in their lives through dishonoring dignitaries and don't know how to break free. Here is a prayer to resolve this issue.

PRAYER OF FREEDOM

Lord Jesus, forgive me for dishonoring those in authority _____ *(name those whom the Holy Spirit brings to remembrance). You are the ultimate authority and require us to submit to those You've placed as authorities in our lives. I repent for the sin of dishonor. Please cancel any curses that dishonor may have opened the door to, and clean my bloodline now, in Jesus' name!*

6. CURSED THROUGH IDOLATRY

I wanted to make this particular sin number one, but I thought it might be cliché to do so, as many books on generational curses start with idolatry. The goal of this book is to have you consider sins that produce curses you've never heard of before. Because of the severity of this sin, I've included it here. Idolatry will always open you to a generational curse. This is how much heaven despises it— and why it is listed in the Ten Commandments: "You shall not make for yourself a carved image...[nor] bow down to them" (Exod. 20:4–5, NKJV). Idolatry was Israel's number one transgression, and today it's still the believer's number one stumbling block, as anything can become an idol to us.

Anything that takes a place in our lives that should only belong to God is *idolatry*. I don't think we need to further elaborate on this, as we are all aware of the severity and consequences of idolatry.

> You must not make for yourself an idol of any kind or an image of anything in the heavens or on the earth or in the sea. You must not bow down to them or worship them, for I, the LORD your God, am a jealous God who will not tolerate your affection for any other gods. I lay the sins of the parents upon their children; the entire family is affected—even children in the third and fourth generations of those who reject me.
>
> —EXODUS 20:4–5

PRAYER OF FREEDOM

Heavenly Father, please forgive my bloodline for all the idolatry we may have participated in through the years. I repent for the sin of idolatry. Please revoke all generational curses we may have initiated. Holy Spirit, cleanse our bloodline with the precious blood of Jesus. I make a covenant right now that I will never worship idols, for You will be the only God I serve for the rest of my days—in Jesus' name!

Now let's look at where curses originate so we can begin to go deeper.

WHERE DO CURSES ORIGINATE?

1. Guardians (Gen. 9)

The first place where humans get cursed is through guardianship, meaning those who have been assigned to raise us until we grow older. These guardians are either our parents, other family members, or various agencies that take us in when our parents abandon us (boarding schools, adoption agencies, etc.). A child is molded from the time they are born until the age of five, and it's during those years that words of affirmation, love, and acceptance crucially imprint that child and help them grow up to be a healthy human being. But when the assigned guardians curse with either their words or their actions, these individuals, years later, end up in front of me going through deliverance.

I've conducted countless deliverance sessions, and the demons that attached themselves through these curses by the person's guardians always show up. They show up so frequently that I usually confront the demons attached to word curses first, and it never fails—the most vile and ugly demons show up. Look at how Noah cursed his grandson Canaan for the sin of his father, Ham. This curse extended itself for many generations until the children of Israel completely wiped out the nation of Canaan.

> When Noah awoke from his drunken stupor, and learned what had happened and what Ham, his younger son, had done, he cursed Ham's descendants: "A curse upon the Canaanites," he swore.

> "May they be the lowest of slaves to the descendants of Shem and Japheth."
>
> —GENESIS 9:24–25, TLB

The future of all people is usually tied to the words of those who are their guardians. This is why it's important that you speak life over your children, over your families, and over all who are under your care.

2. Spiritual high rank (Josh. 9:23)

The next group of people that can either bless or curse are those who have been given spiritual oversight and authority over people. When a person has been sanctioned by God to be a spiritual leader over His people, the responsibility comes with the ability to speak blessing and cursing over people's lives. In the following passage you will see just how powerful the words of Jacob were. Why? Because Jacob was considered a patriarch during the formation of the nation of Israel. He held an immense amount of authority as a patriarch because he was needed to help produce the lineage of the promised Messiah.

One day Jacob decided to leave his father-in-law, Laban, and right before they left, his wife Rachel (Laban's daughter) took her father's idols—we're not told why. When her father discovered that his idols were missing, he pursued Jacob until he found him.

> So one day while Laban was out shearing sheep, Jacob set his wives and sons on camels, and fled without telling Laban his intentions. He drove the flocks before him—Jacob's flocks he had

gotten there at Paddan-aram—and took everything he owned and started out to return to his
father Isaac in the land of Canaan. So he fled
with all of his possessions (and Rachel stole her
father's household gods and took them with her)
and crossed the Euphrates River and headed for
the territory of Gilead....

"But see here—though you feel you must go,
and long so intensely for your childhood home—
why have you stolen my idols?"

"I sneaked away because I was afraid," Jacob
answered. "I said to myself, 'He'll take his daugh-
ters from me by force.' But as for your household idols, a curse upon anyone who took them.
Let him die! If you find a single thing we've stolen from you, I swear before all these men, I'll
give it back without question." For Jacob didn't
know that Rachel had taken them. Laban went
first into Jacob's tent to search there, then into
Leah's, and then searched the two tents of the
concubines, but didn't find them. Finally he
went into Rachel's tent. Rachel, remember, was
the one who had stolen the idols; she had stuffed
them into her camel saddle and now was sitting
on them! So although Laban searched the tents
thoroughly, he didn't find them.

—GENESIS 31:17–21, 30–34, TLB

As you can see from the story, Jacob became enraged
at his father-in-law's accusation and pronounced a cursed
on anyone who happened to take the idols. Without his

realizing it, Jacob's beloved wife Rachel had taken them. The curse of death was now activated over Rachel's life. Years passed, and during the birth of their last child, Benjamin, the curse of death came upon Rachel, and she died during childbirth. Jacob did not know his words held that much authority in the courtroom of heaven.

> Leaving Bethel, he and his household traveled on toward Ephrath (Bethlehem). But Rachel's pains of childbirth began while they were still a long way away. After a very hard delivery, the midwife finally exclaimed, "Wonderful—another boy!" And with Rachel's last breath (for she died) she named him "Ben-oni" ("Son of my sorrow"); but his father called him "Benjamin" ("Son of my right hand"). So Rachel died, and was buried near the road to Ephrath (also called Bethlehem).
> —GENESIS 35:16–19, TLB

Our words have power. Time won't allow me to tell of other stories, such as when Elisha cursed the forty-two boys for dishonoring him (2 Kings 2:24), or when Elijah cursed the two groups of soldiers who came to arrest him (2 Kings 1:10). I think I made my point here.

3. Angels from heaven

Angels also have the ability to curse people. We find Gabriel cursing Zechariah because he wouldn't believe the word of the Lord concerning the birth of his son, John (the Baptist). I'm not sure why Gabriel took offense to Zechariah's unbelief, but it was enough to produce a curse of silence on his life until the child was born. The essence of the story is clear: when heaven gives you a directive concerning the future, it's best you obey and not doubt.

> Then the angel said, "I am Gabriel! I stand in the very presence of God. It was he who sent me to you with this good news! And now, because you haven't believed me, you are to be stricken silent, unable to speak until the child is born. For my words will certainly come true at the proper time."
>
> —LUKE 1:19–20, TLB

There are many other instances in Scripture where angels blessed and cursed humans depending upon their responses to the divine directives.

CASES AGAINST HOUSEHOLDS (BLOODLINES)

The case between God and households is all throughout Scripture. Heaven at times has made covenants with certain families. We find God making a covenant with the "household" of David. God also made a covenant with the tribe of Levi and others. These verses also show that God not only makes covenants of blessing with families but also curses. At times God brings charges and cases against people and also their families. Sometimes cases against households can last for multiple generations while the case is going to trial in the courtroom of heaven. I know we don't like to think like this, but these scriptures highlight that this does indeed happen.

> "Therefore, I will bring my case against you," says the LORD. "I will even bring charges against your children's children in the years to come."
> —JEREMIAH 2:9

> And this is what the LORD of Heaven's Armies says: I am sending this curse into the house of every thief and into the house of everyone who swears falsely using my name. And my curse will remain in that house and completely destroy it— even its timbers and stones.
> —ZECHARIAH 5:4

When a person lives a life of thievery, this sin can cause the curse of the Lord to be transferred to their house. Using God's name in vain will produce a curse as well. This curse will also extend itself to the bricks, mortar, and timber that hold the house together.

CONCLUDING THOUGHTS

As we close this chapter, you've come to realize just how the courtroom of heaven views curses, and how they get activated in people's lives. Take what you've learned and begin to appropriate it in your life. Ask the Holy Spirit to prepare you for what you will be learning in the coming chapters.

CHAPTER 5

ALGORITHM AND THE EVOLUTION OF CURSES

But reach out and take away everything he has, and he will surely *curse* you to your face!

—JOB 1:11

His wife said to him, "Are you still trying to maintain your integrity? *Curse* God and die."

—JOB 2:9

At last Job spoke, and he *cursed* the day of his birth.

—JOB 3:1

UNLIKE WHAT RELIGION has taught us—that all sins are equal—Scripture actually teaches that there are degrees of sin and different levels of consequences. In this chapter we will look at the *algorithm* and *evolution* of sin and curses, words most people are familiar with in this digital age. But first let's define them.

Algorithm—a sequence of well-defined instructions, typically to solve a class of problems or to perform a computation. A step-by-step procedure for calculations.[1]

Evolution—change in the gene pool of a population from generation to generation by such processes as mutation, natural selection, and genetic drift. A process of gradual, peaceful, progressive change or development, as in social or economic structure or institutions.[2]

Everything is controlled by information. From the day we are born to the day we die, we are always learning by a continual stream of information. We read books, we go to school, we listen to teachers, we constantly look things up on the internet, and we read manuals for the items we purchase. Everything hinges on this one thing: *data* and the understanding and documenting of it.

The same is true in the courtroom of heaven. The Bible says that one day we will all give an account for every idle word, which means when you stand before God, "the books" will be opened and all the information documented in those books will determine your heavenly reward and losses (Rev. 20:12). Even your salvation depends on information and documentation, because if your name is not written in the Lamb's Book of Life then you cannot enter the kingdom of God.

Without getting too deep, this whole idea of *data*, information, and documentation is fascinating and can be used to help us understand how sin evolves and how curses are determined and resolved. This is why the Bible encourages us to make it a daily discipline to read the Word of God, because "man shall not live on bread alone, but by every word that comes from the mouth of God" (Matt. 4:4, ESV). Continually filling ourselves with the Word will cause us to have the needed information of what God desires for us, what to use against the enemy when he is tempting and attacking us, and how to govern our lives in a way that pleases God.

In recent years there has been so much emphasis on information/data that multibillion-dollar sciences are built around it to help IT companies understand how it works and how to use it efficiently in today's society. Just a couple of decades ago everything had to be written, and people were given the job of analyzing data (data analysts). Now there is no need for such positions, as technology has advanced to the point where computers do the analyzing for us with quantum computing, algorithm, and artificial intelligence.[3] Nonliving machines are actually solving the problems of life simply by analyzing information. This information allows them to know what data programming needs to be made, and this analyzation of data is called *algorithm*!

Algorithm is a system that calculates data and determines a move you're probably going to make based on that information. Put in real-world vernacular, it determines what your likes and dislikes are and determines the "probability" of what you're going to do based on past actions. If this isn't a metaphor about generational curses then I don't know what is. Heaven can determine the move your family is going to make based on past moves they've already made. We see this behavior all the time as we scroll through the internet and see ads along the sides of the web pages we browse, promoting different products for us to buy.

The kingdom of darkness knows how to use data to its favor and which "ads" to offer us as a temptation to the soul. Satan knows which sins to present to us because he knows, based on past data, which ones our family bloodline will choose. Every family has proclivities that are tailor-made specifically to cause their household to fall.

When I looked up how algorithm is calculated and determined, I rejoiced because what I discovered fits in exactly with what this chapter covers. Please see this through the lens of prototypes (as discussed in chapter 1 of *The Secrets to Deliverance*). Algorithm is determined by three things:

- Average cases
- Best cases
- Worst cases

These three levels help determine what is the highest and lowest probability. Average case means there is average probability (based on data) that a particular pattern of behavior is possible. Worst case means the probability of a particular action is extremely low. And best case means the highest probability is available and will likely occur. I believe the kingdom of darkness has been gathering information on humans since the beginning of time, and it knows the highest and lowest probability of what will cause us to sin and open a door to a curse.

HOW SIN, THE CURSE, AND WICKEDNESS EVOLVE

If you read closely in the Book of Job, you will see the progression of blasphemy trying to enter Job's life. You first see Satan telling God that if He removes all the blessings He has allowed Job to have, Job will curse Him. When that doesn't work, we find Job's wife telling him to curse God and die. Finally, when Job can't handle any more hits, when he is at the lowest, he doesn't curse God but actually curses himself.

I must stress that the contents of this chapter in no way glorify the power of evil or take away the efficacy of Christ's work on the cross. With the overload of information on the kingdom of darkness it may appear that we're taking away the efficacy and power of the Word of God. Trust me, we are not—for Jesus became the curse.

> But Christ has rescued us from the curse pronounced by the law. When he was hung on the cross, he took upon himself the curse for our wrongdoing. For it is written in the Scriptures, "Cursed is everyone who is hung on a tree."
>
> —GALATIANS 3:13

Jesus broke "the curse's" power, and now all believers can appropriate what Jesus did on the cross and walk in total victory.

MULTITUDE OF INIQUITIES

Can sin evolve? Scripture is clear that it does. We see this as far back as the fall of Lucifer. The Scripture describes the fall of Lucifer as a slow progression of evil. He didn't decide to lead a rebellion one day. It was a slow evolving of evil that grew in his heart. We don't know exactly when this happened or the details of what led to Satan's rebellion, but we're told enough to know that sin multiplied and one sin led to another. Vanity led to pride, then pride led to rebellion, rebellion led to manipulation, manipulation led to insurrection, and insurrection led to his banishment. The following verse actually says that evil can grow in multitudes.

> Thou hast defiled thy sanctuaries by the *multitude* of thine iniquities [plural], by the iniquity of thy traffick; therefore will I bring forth a fire from the midst of thee, it shall devour thee, and I will bring thee to ashes upon the earth in the sight of all them that behold thee.
>
> —EZEKIEL 28:18, KJV

It was very clear to the prophet Ezekiel through the Holy Spirit that the cause of Satan's fall was that his sins multiplied to the point of no return. It's very easy to repent and break free from one sin, extremely quick to realize you're wrong when you commit one sin, but when you're overwhelmed with many sins, it becomes more difficult, as your love for obedience grows cold and you find yourself in the place of deception.

> Sin will be rampant everywhere, and the love of many will grow cold.
>
> —MATTHEW 24:12

Paul also addressed this when he wrote to Timothy concerning a group of people who never allowed themselves to be held accountable nor grow in the knowledge they already had (or had been learning); they jumped from teaching to teaching. The reason is very clear: they were *laden* with many sins. That word *laden* means heavily burdened and weighed down. The ultimate end is persons, families, and bloodlines being led away captive to various lusts.

> For of this sort are they which creep into houses,
> and lead captive silly women *laden* with sins, led
> away with divers lusts.
> —2 TIMOTHY 3:6, KJV

But the good news is that Jesus came to set the captives free and break the power of all curses. Let's dive deeper into this topic.

THE HEAVENLY BANK ACCOUNT

There is such a huge hidden secret in this segment regarding generational blessings (the same can be applied to generational curses) that I want to provide insight into some Scripture passages that have been seen in a different light. This "secret" has to do with our heavenly "bank account," and for reference let's turn to the story of Solomon building the temple.

King Solomon was the wisest man who ever lived, and during his reign he led Israel to reach the highest peak of its existence. We find many kings (royals) wanting to be in alliance with Solomon but also desiring to hear his wisdom, including the Queen of Sheba. The temple Solomon built was the most glorious temple in the whole Middle East dedicated to the God of Jacob. Solomon's wisdom far exceeded that of any kings before or after him. Yet most people don't know that none of his achievements would have been possible had it not been for his father, David.

During his earthly battles David accumulated enough wealth and resources that all Solomon needed to do was use what his father left him access to in his treasuries. The wealth inherited by Solomon was not only enough to build the temple without needing much outside help, but David also left him the blueprint of how to build it. All Solomon needed to do was follow the instructions from his father.

> Then King David turned to the entire assembly and said, "My son Solomon, whom God has clearly chosen as the next king of Israel, is still young and inexperienced. The work ahead of him is enormous, for the Temple he will build is not for mere mortals—it is for the LORD God himself! Using every resource at my command, I have gathered as much as I could for building the Temple of my God. Now there is enough gold, silver, bronze, iron, and wood, as well as great quantities of onyx, other precious stones, costly jewels, and all kinds of fine stone and marble. And now, because of my devotion to the Temple of my God, I am giving all of my own private treasures of gold and silver to help in the construction. This is in addition to the building materials I have already collected for his holy Temple."
>
> —1 CHRONICLES 29:1–3

What an example for us to follow as leaders of our families! Throughout the years many people have asked me,

"Pagani, why do you go so hard for God?" And my response is usually the same: "Someone in my bloodline lived for God so zealously that a covenant was made with God and that person that their bloodline would always serve God just like them." My second response is, "I'm going to live so hard for God that future generations in the Pagani bloodline will receive the benefits."

When the Bible says that on that day we will all give an "account" (see Romans 14:12 and Revelation 20:12), it means that for every person born on the earth there is an account, a record, in which everything is documented about our lives. The Bible calls this "the books," in which is our heavenly bank account from which we can make withdrawals during times of great need. This is why many times when the Israelites were in crisis, their kings would remind God of all the things they had done and wanted it deposited in the treasuries. Look what Nehemiah said:

> Then I commanded the Levites to purify them-
> selves and to guard the gates in order to pre-
> serve the holiness of the Sabbath. Remember
> this good deed also, O my God! Have compas-
> sion on me according to your great and unfail-
> ing love....Remember them, O my God, for they
> have defiled the priesthood and the solemn vows
> of the priests and Levites....I also made sure that
> the supply of wood for the altar and the first por-
> tions of the harvest were brought at the proper
> times. Remember this in my favor, O my God.
> —NEHEMIAH 13:22, 29, 31

Here's the astounding news: when even one person lives in a godly manner, it gets credited to the household. And future generations find their lives a lot easier because of the generations before them. Look how easy it was for Solomon to finish building the temple.

> So Solomon finished all his work on the Temple of the LORD. Then he brought all the gifts his father, David, had dedicated—the silver, the gold, and the various articles—and he stored them in the treasuries of the Temple of God.
>
> —2 CHRONICLES 5:1

Jesus reminded us of this principle when He said, "Store up for yourselves treasures in heaven" (Matt. 6:19–20, NIV). The average American Evangelical will read this verse as meaning "rewards." But rewards aren't needed in heaven. They are needed on earth. The text actually says treasures. These deposits are stored in our accounts for future use.

> Store your treasures in heaven, where moths and rust cannot destroy, and thieves do not break in and steal. Wherever your treasure is, there the desires of your heart will also be.
>
> —MATTHEW 6:20–21

A biblical example of this can be found in the life of a Roman centurion called Cornelius in Acts 10. The text says that because of his good deeds in helping various synagogues, there was a memorial in heaven that caused God to send a blessing to his bloodline (v. 4).

Just know that what you do in this life is being stored up in heaven for the next generation to make a withdrawal. Make a decision right now to seek the Lord so zealously that your future generations will receive the benefit. The Bible says that when Abram blessed Melchizedek with a tithe of all he had won from the spoils, he received a blessing. Hebrews 7:9 (KJV) goes into more detail on this, saying that Abram's great-grandson Levi gave tithes "in" Abraham—meaning that though Levi wasn't born until two generations later, it was credited to his account.

This revelation can also be seen when someone lives in sin. Their storehouses in heaven are filled with violence, rebellion, and witchcraft. Sadly, we can expect to see much calamity in such families.

Ask the Holy Spirit right now to empower you with *zeal* to stir up the gift of God within so that you begin to make heavenly deposits for your bloodline!

I'm hoping at this point you're beginning to see things from a legal perspective and how the courtroom of heaven plays a vital role in our everyday lives. Jesus emphasized this in His model prayer when He said, "Thy kingdom come, Thy will be done" (Matt. 6:10, KJV)—implying that this kingdom constitution must be obeyed and enforced. Which leads to the next thing we want to discuss—namely, the laws, regulations, and stipulations of this kingdom and the penalties for not obeying. We can't obey a command we don't know exists, and we won't obey that command if we aren't aware of the penalties and consequences for not obeying.

As I mentioned at the start of this chapter, there are

different degrees of sin, and some may initiate a generational curse while others may not. Let me explain.

DEGREES OF SIN

Sins are not all the same. It is widely preached, taught, and accepted that all sin carries the same penalty, but this is not a true biblical model. The following verse is one of the most revolutionizing passages I have ever read regarding this. Not all sin leads to hell, and not all sin leads to eternal condemnation nor initiates a generational curse. If you look closely at the following verse, it clearly says that not all sins lead to death, defined as eternal separation from the presence of God.

> If any man see his brother sin a sin which is not unto death, he shall ask, and he shall give him life for them that sin not unto death. There is a sin unto death: I do not say that he shall pray for it. All unrighteousness is sin: and there is a sin not unto death.
>
> —1 JOHN 5:16–17, KJV

Here's an example to help you better understand this verse. If I have an argument with my wife, though it's a sin, it will *not* produce a generational curse. But if I commit adultery against her, it *will* produce a curse. The consequence will depend on the severity of the sin. The apostle John knew this and stressed it in his epistle. There is a progression of sin. The courtroom of heaven has categorized this progression by the sins below.

1. Violation (unintentional)—"a breach, infringement, or transgression, as of a law, rule, promise, etc.; desecration; profanation."[4]

The pathway to sin always begins with a violation, an act of being irreverent concerning what God has outlined in His law. Violations are the entryway for committing larger and more severe sins. Everything starts as a simple violation. Most violations are small and don't carry a severe punishment. But if committed frequently, they will lead a person to commit graver sins that might lead to breaking God's law. Violations are not sin but rather indiscretions toward the law of God.

The act of violating implies unintentional wrongdoing, yet not enough to warrant anything more than a fine, a verbal chastisement, or a citation. In the Old Testament many offerings the priests made on behalf of the people were for nothing more than violations to the law. Most payment for violations never required blood sacrifices but only payments made in shekels or smaller animals, such as doves. When a person has been caught committing this infraction, there usually is only a conviction of the Holy Spirit and encouragement to never do it again. But if the believer continues, it will lead to sin.

2. Sin—missing the mark; falling short; this is *unintentional* disobedience expressed through our sinful nature passed down to us through the fall of mankind. There's no way of escape until the glorification of our human bodies.

When a believer crosses the threshold of violation and enters the realm of sin, things begin on a totally different nature. Sin is wrong. Though not malicious at times, it's still wrong, and it displeases the Lord.

The Book of James says that sin, the result of our sinful nature inherited from Adam, is in direct opposition to God. Our flesh tempts us to sin, and without resistance we fall into it.

> Temptation comes from our own desires, which entice us and drag us away. These desires give birth to sinful actions. And when sin is allowed to grow, it gives birth to death.
>
> —James 1:14–15

Paul explains a bit more in detail about the sinful nature when he says, "What I desire to do I don't, and what I hate, I find myself doing" (Rom. 7:19), which in essence means that our sinful nature is already bent on fulfilling its own evil desire, with or without our permission. It's here that heaven is merciful and understands but still requires us to resist all temptation. But committing sinful acts might not necessarily cause there to be a judgment or a generational curse.

When you move beyond the sin level to transgression, now you're treading on dangerous territory. Let's look more closely at transgression.

3. **Transgression**—the Hebrew word *pasha* means "to rebel, transgress, revolt";[5] it implies a breach of trust. This is the *willful* and *intentional* disobedience that a person chooses, even after being given a way of escape. They choose

to breach that trust—to intentionally disobey, to willfully trespass.

> Dear friends, if we *willfully* continue sinning after we have received knowledge of the truth, there is no longer any sacrifice that will cover these sins. There is only the terrible expectation of God's judgment and the raging fire that will consume his enemies.
>
> —HEBREWS 10:26–27

The Scripture is clear; when a person begins to commit transgression or live in open transgression, it's usually the result of willful disobedience and will always produce judgment. Actually, the verse says *you can expect* this judgment. At this level, transgression has the potential to initiate a generational curse and leads to iniquity.

4. Iniquity—a premeditated choice with no regard for consequence or repentance, resulting in the modifying of the genetics (nature) of the persons giving themselves over to such sins.

If you engage in unrepentant transgression for long periods of time, it becomes iniquity. At this level the person's nature changes, and they start to embody and become this particular transgression to the point where it's second nature. Iniquity has the power to alter one's DNA and cause a person to become the sin that dominates them.[6] We can see this in 2 Thessalonians where Paul says the Antichrist will be called the Mystery of Iniquity, meaning he will be the living embodiment of the devil—literally Satan walking among us.

> You are of your father the devil, and the desires
> of your father you want to do [carry his nature
> and DNA].
>
> —JOHN 8:44, NKJV

During the time of Christ the Israelites had a hard time receiving His ministry, not because it was difficult to discern but because they had lived for so long in rebellion to God's law that their very nature had embraced that of the devil—so Jesus called them out on it. He told them they were children of the devil. This wasn't just a metaphor but rather an identification. Throughout my years of ministry, I've met persons and families so steeped in sin and iniquity that there was little to no room for any gospel presentation. At this point a generational curse has begun, and many times such families die in sin and end up spending an eternity away from God.

5. Abomination—that which is loathed or detested and therefore utterly offensive to the Lord.

This fifth level of sin is the most loathed by God and *only* produces a generational curse, 100 percent of the time. It is here where a person doesn't care and commits acts that even God Himself finds detestable. Various sins are considered abominations; such sins are *hated* by God, and about them He will never change His mind. What's interesting is that many of these sins are things modern civilization takes pride in committing the most. Here are some examples of sin that Scripture condemns:

- Homosexuality
- Bestiality
- Abortion
- Incest

> Ye shall therefore keep my statutes and my judgments, and shall not commit any of these *abominations*; neither any of your own nation, nor any stranger that sojourneth among you.
>
> —LEVITICUS 18:26, KJV

Before we close out this chapter and move into degrees of disobedience, the topic of the next chapter, let me state categorically that all abominations produce curses. This is sobering stuff, and anyone who enters this level of sin is playing with fire.

CHAPTER 6

DEGREES OF DISOBEDIENCE, LEVELS OF UNCLEANNESS

I BELIEVE DISOBEDIENCE IS the reason why the church and many believers are so defeated or don't receive answers to prayers. Disobedience isn't singular; it's a category that encompasses a wide range of sins. Many of them we know, and others we've glanced over when reading Scripture.

The Bible says, "My people are destroyed for lack of knowledge" (Hos. 4:6, ESV), but the verse goes on to say, "because you have rejected knowledge." This rejection usually comes in the form of not taking the time to study and pursue more understanding of the things of God. If disobedience has more than one definition for the act of it, then it's imperative we find out what those other definitions are so we don't violate the terms of sanctification and the covenant of holiness out of ignorance.

Many of you may think the following forms of disobedience are all the same thing, but they are not. When you study the meaning of *forget*, for example, you will see it is not the same thing as *abandon* or *forsake*. *Rejection* has a whole different feel to it. In keeping with these distinctions, they don't all carry the same penalties or consequences, but all are still either mild or severe forms of disobedience, and some of them can actually produce a generational curse.

1. FORGETTING

What comes to mind when you think of the phrase "to forget"? One of the first things I think of is that it might not have been intentional. How many times have we awakened from sleep and forgotten we promised the Lord that today we would fast and seek Him? And we went out and ordered breakfast, and in the middle of breakfast we realized we had totally forgotten about our vow or promise. Was our forgetfulness intentional? It depends, but more than likely it was not. Regardless of the intention, it can still be wrong, depending on the severity of the situation. Let's look at the following verse:

> My people are destroyed for lack of knowledge; because you have rejected knowledge, I reject you from being a priest to me. And since you have *forgotten* the law of your God, I also will forget your children.
>
> —HOSEA 4:6, ESV

The Hebrew words for *forget* are *shakach* and *nashah*. They mean "to ignore, neglect, forsake, or to act in disregard."[1] Out of all those definitions, I believe the one that sticks out the most is "ignore." When you ignore something, it means it isn't the most important thing on your mind. Not that it isn't on your mind; it's just not the most important thing on your mind. And whatever is not the most important is easily overlooked and forgotten in moments of crisis.

Forgetting about something doesn't mean it's not important. Again, it just means it's not the *most* important. I'm sure the priests during the time of Isaiah had the Law of Moses in mind, but they didn't have it in their hearts, so in moments when they should have been obedient, they disobeyed. Mild disobedience is still disobedience but doesn't carry the penalty of a generational curse. However, it does cause heaven to deal with you within the law of reciprocity, meaning you will reap what you sow.

We find this all over Scripture. "Draw near to God, and he will draw near to you" (Jas. 4:8, ESV). In the Hosea text we just read, God said (paraphrased), "You forgot Me, so I will forget you." This is why the Lord told the children of Israel, "Write [My commandments] on the doorposts of your house and on your gates" (Deut. 6:9). I'm sure if God was telling them to write His commandments on their doorposts, it's because humans forget quite frequently. We find many verses in the Book of Psalms where David says, "I won't forget Your law," or "Keep Your laws ever before me." Reminders keep you in a state of constant remembrance and always ready to obey.

Moments of deep need when it seems the heavens are brass could genuinely be the result of a person getting exactly what they have been giving to God. Ask yourself, "Am I forgetting the law of the Lord in my daily living?" If so, make every effort to keep yourself in a place of constant remembrance.

2. ABANDONING

Abandoning carries the same intention as forgetting. Not all abandonment is malicious and done with bad intentions.

When a single mother becomes pregnant at an early age and abandons her child to an adoption agency, the intention is not malicious but rather protective. The mother knows she is too young to care for a child, so she hands her child over to parents who can take of it. This act of handing over is really called *relinquishing*. If you look closely at the Hebrew word for *abandon, âzaḇ*—a primitive root—it means to loosen or relinquish.[2] The idea is to hand out or loosen. When you loosen something, it means you lose a tight grip on it or let it go. The following verse shows that King Rehoboam loosened his grip on the law of the Lord, and so did Israel with him.

> When the rule of Rehoboam was established and
> he was strong, he *abandoned* the law of the LORD,
> and all Israel with him.
> —2 CHRONICLES 12:1, ESV

This type of disobedience falls along the lines of carelessness, because normally when someone loosens their grip it means they're holding something that is important and valuable. If I am holding a glass, because of its fragile nature it's best I don't loosen my grip, as I'm likely to have it slip from my hands and break. When a believer relinquishes the Law of Moses, they end up sinning by not keeping a firm grip. This happens a lot when God starts blessing His people. Over time they forget who blessed them and where they came from, and soon they start loosening up in many of the rules and regulations that actually got them to that level. Success is often the reason for those who abandon

God. Abandoning, though a sin, doesn't cause a generational curse. But it will cause God to extend His chastening hand and take away some of the blessing He gave, to cause them to repent.

3. FORSAKING

When believers enter the realm of forsaking, they're entering dangerous territory. This particular form of disobedience can open the door to the demonic. It's one thing to forget or abandon the law of the Lord, but when a Christian starts forsaking it, doors open that can cause havoc in their lives—and forsaking means it was an intentional action. When someone forsakes something, for whatever reason, the act is intentional! The Hebrew word for *forsake* (*âzab*) means "to leave, abandon, forsake, neglect, apostatize."[3] Look at the following verse:

> And the LORD says: "Because they have *forsaken*
> my law that I set before them, and have not
> obeyed my voice or walked in accord with it..."
> —JEREMIAH 9:13, ESV

What I find dangerous about forsaking is that the word *apostatize* is included in its meaning. When a believer apostatizes, it means they *leave the faith* they once embraced, or they leave the things that matter and embrace other things that don't matter. Many leave the faith and embrace witchcraft, or they may go to another religion. This act of disobedience will cause all kinds of judgments from heaven but doesn't necessarily cause a generational curse. But the last two we are about to mention will.

4. REJECTING

At this point, there's no way around it. The word *reject* means to despise or refuse. This word alone implies that someone knows the truth full well and knows what God is demanding with it, yet still refuses to obey it. And heaven places this category on the same level as witchcraft. "For rebellion is as the sin of witchcraft" (1 Sam. 15:23, KJV). This is why when a person—especially a believer—rejects following God's laws and ways, it will always produce a generational curse. Look what the text says:

> Thus says the LORD: "For three transgressions of Judah, and for four, I will not revoke the punishment, because they have rejected the law of the LORD."
>
> —AMOS 2:4, ESV

All throughout Scripture, whenever the children of Israel rejected God's law, it always resulted in banishment, exile, or judgment. The lasting effects of this judgment always went beyond the offender to their children and their children's children. God promised that all who disobeyed Him at this level would not walk away guiltless; He would transfer a curse unto the third and fourth generations.

5. DOING VIOLENCE AGAINST

This last level of disobedience is the most obvious that will cause generational curses to be activated in a person's life. The word *violence* means to do wrong, do violence to, treat violently, do wrongly. This offense happens when a person has gotten to the point where they not only reject the law of the Lord, they also do violence against it—meaning they assault the Word in trying to alter what it says or means, or they attack anyone who tries to obey and believe in it. We find this many times with those who once served the Lord, and for whatever reason, they depart from the faith and begin a campaign to discredit the Bible and the ways of the Lord. They make it their vendetta to shipwreck the faith of those seeking truth.

> Her prophets are fickle, treacherous men; her priests profane what is holy; they do *violence* to the law.
>
> —ZEPHANIAH 3:4, ESV

The text is clear that the priests do violence against the law. We're seeing an assault on the Word of God in our age with various mainline denominations who once held to the authority of Scripture and are now trying to alter it by ordaining homosexual bishops, promoting the pro-choice agenda in their pulpits, and adhering to New Age practices in their teachings. The Bible is clear in the Book of Jude where it says, concerning false teachers who distort God's Word, "[their] condemnation was written about long ago" (v. 4, NIV).

THESECRETS TO GENERATIONAL CURSES

LEVELS OF UNCLEANNESS

Not only are there different degrees of sin and different levels
of evil, but there are also different degrees of moral sins that
affect a person's character and personality. There are times
when a person can live in sin but not be a bad person; they
are just entangled in the web of sin. But then there are times
when it's not just an entanglement—the person is morally
wrong. The following can be found all throughout Scripture
in different instances, but I want you to see the progression
and its evolution. Without getting too detailed, I've attached
some Bible verses next to each level of uncleanness to help
give further definition. I believe they're self-explanatory and
don't need further insight except to define what they mean.

**1. Defiled—"a primitive root; to be foul, especially in a
ceremonial or moral sense (contaminated)"[4]**

> Now the sons of Reuben the firstborn of Israel, (for
> he was the firstborn; but forasmuch as he defiled
> his father's bed, his birthright was given unto the
> sons of Joseph the son of Israel: and the genealogy
> is not to be reckoned after the birthright).
> —1 CHRONICLES 5:1, KJV

**2. Contaminated—affected by contamination, "the
act of contaminating or polluting; including (either
intentionally or accidentally) unwanted substances or
factors"[5]**

> Rescue others by snatching them from the flames
> of judgment. Show mercy to still others, but do so

with great caution, hating the sins that contaminate their lives.

—JUDE 23

3. Unclean—"having a physical or moral blemish so as to make impure according to...dietary or ceremonial laws"[6]

> Wherefore come out from among them, and be ye separate, saith the Lord, and touch not the unclean thing; and I will receive you.
>
> —2 CORINTHIANS 6:17, KJV

4. Corrupted—brought to "a degenerate state, debased state, prevention, invalid state, putrid state, spoiled, fainted, vitiates and unsound experience"[7]

> Everything is pure to those whose hearts are pure. But nothing is pure to those who are corrupt and unbelieving, because their minds and consciences are corrupted.
>
> —TITUS 1:15

THE THREE WORST BLOODLINES IN ISRAEL'S HISTORY

Let's further drive this point of the different degrees and levels of sins by showing you three different bloodlines that were sinful, extremely evil, and most abominable. When a family's willful alignment with evil is so pervasive, eventually God Himself steps in and says, "No more!"

Though there are many households and bloodlines in

Scripture that the Lord hated, three ended up being the worst, where God made it His personal mission to wipe the memory of them from the face of the earth. They are the household of Jeroboam, the family of Baasha, and the bloodline of Josiah. I want to take a few moments to explain these three bloodlines and allow them to serve as warning so we can make sure we guide our families to living lives that please God.

THE HOUSEHOLD OF JEROBOAM

This particular king is not one of the more popular kings within Judeo-Christianity. Other evil kings and queens such as Ahab and Jezebel seem to take all the spotlight. And while those other kings did receive the same fate as Jeroboam, I don't think there was anyone more overlooked yet more evil than Jeroboam. He is the perfect example of someone given over to the opinions of the people. He would do whatever it took not to lose his influence over the people—even causing the Israelites to embrace idolatry.

Jeroboam was the son of Nebat and lived during the reign of King Solomon. He was part of Solomon's workforce and quickly moved up the ranks to gain more authority. It was during this time that Solomon backslid from serving the Lord, and the Lord sent the prophet Ahijah to tell him that heaven was stripping the nation away from him (Solomon) and only allowing two tribes to remain under his control; the other ten would be given to Jeroboam.

During Jeroboam's reign Israel prospered for a season, and one day he became afraid that the ten tribes would turn back to Solomon during the feasts and pilgrimages required by God. He set up his own version of the worship of YHWH by erecting two golden calves, one at the top of the kingdom and one at the bottom. So instead of having to make the journey to the southern kingdom in Jerusalem, the worshippers attended Jeroboam's version of the religion of Israel. The end result was that the northern kingdom turned to deep idolatry that no other king would be able to remove.

The following verse describes why God chose to curse the bloodline of Jeroboam.

> For the children of Israel walked in all the sins of Jeroboam which he did; they departed not from them.
>
> —2 KINGS 17:22, KJV

The sins of Jeroboam were so hard to remove that God had to prophesy the coming of a man named Josiah (2 Kings 23:15–20) who would bring the nation through a reformation and finally remove these sins. So the prophet Ahijah, who anointed King Jeroboam, now pronounced a generational curse against his household.

> You have done more evil than all who lived before you. You have made other gods for yourself and have made me furious with your gold calves. And since you have turned your back on me, I will bring disaster on your dynasty and will destroy every one of your male descendants, slave and free alike, anywhere in Israel. I will burn up your

royal dynasty as one burns up trash until it is all
gone. The members of Jeroboam's family who die
in the city will be eaten by dogs, and those who
die in the field will be eaten by vultures. I, the
LORD, have spoken.

—1 KINGS 14:9–11, 13

This passage of Scripture should stand as a clear warning
that when God raises someone up and grants them authority, they are to be careful to walk according to all the ways
of the Lord. If not, the same God who anoints is the One
who will take them out.

THE HOUSEHOLD OF BAASHA

King Baasha succeeded King Nadab, who succeeded
Jeroboam. He was the great-grandson of King Solomon,
and he assassinated his way to the throne by killing Nadab.
Without realizing it, King Baasha was fulfilling God's will
in wanting to remove King Nadab from the throne. Scripture records that Baasha did what was evil in the sight of
the Lord. He is also known for destroying every trace of
the lineage of King Jeroboam, which in some regards is
what heaven wanted. But the error that caused his demise
was that he allowed the sins Jeroboam instituted to continue, and as a result God decreed the same fate to Baasha
and his dynasty as He did to Jeroboam.

In the following passage you see God pronouncing judgment not just on Baasha but also on his children. This
shows how much God hated the sins of Jeroboam and

how He was looking for a king to bring reformation to the nation and bring the people back to Himself.

> This message from the LORD was delivered to King Baasha by the prophet Jehu son of Hanani: "I lifted you out of the dust to make you ruler of my people Israel, but you have followed the evil example of Jeroboam. You have provoked my anger by causing my people Israel to sin. So now I will destroy you and your family, just as I destroyed the descendants of Jeroboam son of Nebat. The members of Baasha's family who die in the city will be eaten by dogs, and those who die in the field will be eaten by vultures."
>
> —1 KINGS 16:1–4

Many kings of Israel were evil and didn't serve the Lord. But not all of them received a pronouncement of judgment that would outlast them and continue with their children. When God gives the verdict that a generational curse should be carried out against a household, rest assured that this family did something that warranted it. Not only would Baasha's descendants perish under the judgment of the Lord, but they all would die gruesome deaths.

THE HOUSEHOLD OF JOSIAH (ZEDEKIAH AND JEHOIAKIM)

King Josiah was one of the greatest kings Israel ever had, outside of King David. He was not only prophesied by name to come and bring great reformation to the nation—turning the people away from the sins of Jeroboam—but no one was more zealous to restore the purity of the temple of the Lord. (We will deal in more detail about Josiah in chapter 10.)

Unfortunately, this is not how the story of Josiah ends. During the height of his campaign against idolatry, he went out to war against King Neco, Pharaoh of Egypt, and it cost him his life. As influential as Josiah was with the people, due to his sudden death, he did not have that same influence on his sons, who were to succeed him. We find that his sons Zedekiah, Jehoiachin, and Jehoiakim never served the Lord as their father did but actually returned to the sins of the previous evil king. The prophet Ezekiel, who was living during that time, prophesied that God had had enough of Israel's sins—specifically those of the sons of Josiah— such that He pronounced a curse upon their bloodline and would send the children of Israel into Babylonian captivity.

> Say to them, "This is what the Sovereign LORD says: These actions contain a message for King Zedekiah in Jerusalem and for all the people of Israel." Explain that your actions are a sign to show what will soon happen to them, for they will be driven into exile as captives. "Even Zedekiah will leave Jerusalem at night through a hole in the wall, taking only what he can carry with him. He will cover his face, and his eyes will not see the land he is leaving. Then I will throw my net over him and capture him in my snare. I will bring him to Babylon, the land of the

Babylonians, though he will never see it, and he
will die there."

—EZEKIEL 12:10–13

This prophecy came to pass when the Babylonian empire
sieged Jerusalem and Zedekiah was forced to watch his
children and servants die, before the Babylonians gouged
out his eyes. Here we see God bringing judgment against
his bloodline.

> They captured the king and took him to the king
> of Babylon at Riblah, where they pronounced
> judgment upon Zedekiah. They made Zedekiah
> watch as they slaughtered his sons. Then they
> gouged out Zedekiah's eyes, bound him in bronze
> chains, and led him away to Babylon.
>
> —2 KINGS 25:6–7

ROOT OF JESSE (JESSE TO DAVID TO SOLOMON)

Hidden in the story of King David is the evolution of
sin. It's not easily seen, but many theologians believe the
Scripture hints that King David was possibly conceived as
the result of Jesse having an illicit affair. (Please note that
this segment is presented as mere speculation but is *highly
probable* and helps convey the point I'm trying to make
here.)

The following verse is the basis for this idea:

> Behold, I was shapen in iniquity; and in sin did
> my mother conceive me.
>
> —PSALM 51:5, KJV

It's believed that a lot of David's pessimism resulted from a secret his father, Jesse, was hiding, which is why when Samuel asked to see all of his sons, David wasn't included until the prophet insisted there had to be another son.

> Jesse had seven of his sons pass before Samuel, but Samuel said to him, "The LORD has not chosen these." So he asked Jesse, "Are these all the sons you have?"
>
> "There is still the youngest," Jesse answered. "He is tending the sheep." Samuel said, "Send for him; we will not sit down until he arrives." So he sent for him and had him brought in. He was glowing with health and had a fine appearance and handsome features. Then the LORD said, "Rise and anoint him; this is the one."
>
> —1 SAMUEL 16:10–12, NIV

I've always been intrigued by the fact that in Revelation, Jesus exclaims that He is the "*root* and offspring of David" (22:16, KJV). Why would He say "root" when all other scriptures about Him are in reference to Him being the Son of David? The real root of David was actually Jesse, his father, yet Jesus substitutes David's father and places Himself in his stead. Isaiah 11:1–2 states that out of Jesse's root a branch is coming (which is Christ):

> And there shall come forth a rod out of the stem
> of Jesse, and a Branch shall grow out of his *roots*.
> —ISAIAH 11:1–2, KJV

Now why is this important, and what does it have to do with the evolution of generational curses or with King David's bloodline? What potentially started out as someone's unresolved sin can grow with each generation. If Jesse's struggle with lust in one moment led to him having a child out of wedlock and covering up his secret sin, it's no surprise we find David also struggling through his life with various moments of lust—from having multiple wives to trying to cover up his sin with Bathsheba—such that by the time Solomon was on the scene, he had more than seven hundred wives and concubines. Sin can evolve, and generational curses can evolve. The biblical term *iniquity* means sin and transgression carried out over many years with no intervention to the point where it has become deeply entrenched in the nature of the person and they embody the sin they've been committing.

This leads us to a dominant theme of this book—and perhaps its strongest takeaway: *What you fail to deal with in one generation will grow in the next!*

So when Jesus declared Himself the root of David, He was identifying Himself with the root cause of David's generational curse and breaking it in David's bloodline! Jesus not only identified Himself with the root of David's bloodline, He also called Himself "the offspring," solidifying that He would purge David's future generations coming from His bloodline—leading up until Christ's birth!

This is worth rejoicing over! Because of what Jesus did on the cross, and through His blood, He also identifies your bloodline and breaks the curse. It doesn't matter how sinful your household and bloodline are—Jesus came to break the curse. This is why Acts 16:31 says, "Believe in the Lord Jesus, and you will be saved—you and your household" (NIV). He's not just the root of David, or the root of Jesse, but He is also the root of Pagani, the root of _____ (insert your family name). In its proper context this is referring to God cleansing the bloodline of David to prepare the way for the Messiah, who would be born through his dynasty. But it's safe to say that what Jesus did for the bloodline of Jesse, He desires to do with our bloodlines too. God is in the business of cleansing bloodlines!

BORN INTO CURSES: GENETIC MISFORTUNES

An obvious example of what I mean by "genetic misfortune" is the Kennedy bloodline. In my observation, it seems that almost every person born into the Kennedy bloodline has had some level of misfortune—from both Robert and John F. Kennedy being assassinated, to John F. Kennedy Jr. and his wife being killed in an airplane crash, to many of the Kennedy nephews and cousins dying in freak accidents.

Generational curses can not only have devastating effects for generations to come, but I believe they can affect the bloodline to the point where they alter humans physiologically and genetic defects may present themselves. One case in point is Goliath and his brothers, who were all born with six-digit hands as a result of a cursed bloodline. (See 2 Samuel 21:20.) You may notice that some families seem inclined to have people born with genetic defects. I'm not saying all genetic abnormalities are the result of sin and curses, but there are times when I believe they are. Certainly not all sicknesses and diseases that are passed down from one generation to another are the result of sin, but it's possible that some are. If as you read this you discern that this particular curse might be affecting your bloodline, renounce it and repeat the following prayer. Let's break the generational curse of infirmity and believe heaven for supernatural healing!

PRAYER OF FREEDOM

Heavenly Father, I come before You asking You to break the curse of sickness and disease from my bloodline. I humbly request that You allow the healing virtue of Christ to be released and provide healing for my household. By the authority of Jesus' name, I cancel and revoke all generational curses of infirmity from being transferred down my bloodline and command all demons to release my bloodline now in Jesus' name! Lord Jesus, I humbly request that You apply Your blood and sanctify my household, in Jesus' name! (Keep praying in your own words as the Holy Spirit guides you.)

THE CURSE OF HEZEKIAH'S HOUSEHOLD

Let's look closely at the story of King Hezekiah's sickness. To give context to the story, Hezekiah was sick, and the prophet Isaiah came and gave him a word that his sickness would lead to death in three days. The king then turned his face to the wall and pled his case before the Lord. The Lord heard his prayer and granted him a fifteen-year extension of his life. Now, at face value, it's a wonderful story of mercy and healing. But there was a deeper reason why the Lord was allowing that sickness.

> About that time Hezekiah became deathly ill, and the prophet Isaiah son of Amoz went to visit him. He gave the king this message: "This is what the LORD says: Set your affairs in order, for you are going to die. You will not recover from this illness."
>
> —2 KINGS 20:1

Though King Hezekiah was given an extension of his life, God saw the future of what was evolving in him and his bloodline. Hezekiah was already beginning to make the wrong choices that would cost him future generations, and in fact they did. It's my belief that God was allowing this sickness to grip Hezekiah with death because God saw what was going to happen in the future, and He was trying to stop it.

> Then Isaiah the prophet went to King Hezekiah and asked him, "What did those men want?

Where were they from?" Hezekiah replied, "They came from the distant land of Babylon."

"What did they see in your palace?" Isaiah asked. "They saw everything," Hezekiah replied. "I showed them everything I own—all my royal treasuries." Then Isaiah said to Hezekiah, "Listen to this message from the LORD: The time is coming when everything in your palace—all the treasures stored up by your ancestors until now—will be carried off to Babylon. Nothing will be left, says the LORD. Some of your very own sons will be taken away into exile. They will become eunuchs who will serve in the palace of Babylon's king." Then Hezekiah said to Isaiah, "This message you have given me from the LORD is good." For the king was thinking, "At least there will be peace and security during my lifetime."

—2 KINGS 20:14–19

What causes me to be sure that God was indeed trying to allow Hezekiah's death was that during this fifteen-year extension, Hezekiah had a son and named him Manasseh (we deal more in detail about him in chapter 10). In a nutshell, Manasseh became the worst king Israel ever had, and he reigned the longest.

Hezekiah died, and his son Manasseh became the next king.

—2 KINGS 20:21

> Manasseh was twelve years old when he became
> king, and he reigned in Jerusalem fifty-five years.
> He did what was evil in the LORD's sight, follow-
> ing the detestable practices of the pagan nations
> that the LORD had driven from the land ahead of
> the Israelites.
>
> —2 CHRONICLES 33:1–2

Please hear me: I'm not saying that all sickness and disease are the result of God trying to kill someone, but sometimes God *allows* sickness for some greater good and purpose—like the sickness of Lazarus in John 11:1–4, where Jesus said, "This illness…is for the glory of God, so that the Son of God may be glorified through it." It's my firm belief that heaven saw the bad choices Hezekiah was going to make and also foresaw the birth of the most evil king in Israel's history and was trying to save the nation heartache. God is our Jehovah Rapha (our healer), and if you're sick right now or dealing with the generational curse of sickness, then pray the following prayer and believe God's will to be done.

PRAYER OF FREEDOM

Heavenly Father, You are Jehovah Rapha, the God who heals me. I'm here pleading before Your heavenly court like King Hezekiah, and I'm ask-ing You to have mercy on my bloodline by out-stretching Your mighty hand and healing me of _____ (name the sickness, disease, or illness). *By Your stripes I am healed! May Your healing power flow and break all curses of sickness and disease in my bloodline. Thank You, Lord Jesus, for pleading my case before the heavenly court and being my Advocate. By the power of the Holy Spirit, I command every demon of illness to leave my body now, in Jesus' name! (Keep praying your own words as the Holy Spirit guides you.)*

CURSES OF THE MIND

Since we're on this journey of algorithm, let's explore next what I call the curses of the mind. Without getting too detailed and exhaustive, in recent years I've noticed four areas in which people seem to struggle against demonic oppression and generational curses, with increasing occurrences. They are as follows:

- Confusion
- Seared conscience
- Reprobate mind
- Strong delusion

The Bible encourages us to keep our minds on heavenly things. We are commanded to take every thought captive to the obedience of Christ. As you read Scripture, the Word of God is powerful enough to cause you to have the mind of Christ. The mind is the battlefield, and there is an all-out war for control of it. Television, social media, radio, cell phones, computers, news media, and other people are all out to control your mind or an aspect of your thinking. The pharmaceutical industry is making billions on medicines that can control the way your brain operates. Altogether, this onslaught is causing more people to be affected in their minds than in any previous generation. When you talk to people, especially young people, you sense a deep confusion in the mind, and many times that confusion and other mental issues are spread among their whole family. Let's look at how this evolves.

1. Confusion

The following verse blows me away every time I read it because it affirms the point I made earlier that curses do not come from demons but rather from the courtroom of heaven when someone commits a sin that warrants it. The text says "the LORD Himself" will send not just a curse but *confusion*. I believe that when a person refuses to acknowledge God in all their ways, the Lord allows confusion to become their portion. God is not the author of confusion (1 Cor. 14:33), but He allows it when there is a refusal to walk according to His Word.

Analyze your life right now. Has confusion been part of your life since as far back as you can remember? Ask yourself, "Have I been allowing the Word of God to be my resource?" If not, there is a good chance that confusion might be consuming you as a punishment from heaven.

> The LORD himself will send on you curses, *confusion*, and frustration in everything you do, until

at last you are completely destroyed for doing evil
and abandoning me.

—DEUTERONOMY 28:20

PRAYER OF FREEDOM

*Holy Spirit, I'm sorry for not allowing You to
guide every area of my life, especially my mind.
I'm consumed with confusion right now, and I'm
asking You to set me free. Break the curse of confusion over my life. I repent and ask for forgiveness from the curse of confusion. Today I make
the decision to abide in Your Word and allow it
to be a lamp to my feet and a light to my path.
In Jesus' name I command every demon of confusion operating in my mind to leave now and never
come back!* (Keep praying in your own words
as the Holy Spirit guides you.)

2. Seared conscience

This next level is a bit more serious, as our conscience is
the seat of where we distinguish right from wrong. When
a believer loses their ability to sense the convicting power
of the Word of God and the Holy Spirit, they become
callous—indifferent toward the things of God, indifferent
toward the people of God. Their resistance level toward
sin is lowered, and their fear of the Lord starts dwindling.
The Greek word *kausteriazo* means "burn with a hot iron"
(cauterize, sear), and it results in calloused skin.[8] Whether
your skin is burned or rubbed together for long periods of

time and hardens, you lose the ability to feel pain in that area. The same can be said about a seared conscience; a person has no more feeling of conviction and integrity, so they start speaking lies in hypocrisy and don't even know they're doing it.

Another way to look at this is when we become desensitized to things that used to bother us. If there is one thing you never want to lose it's the presence of the Holy Spirit and hearing His voice. Without His voice, we can end up like King Saul when the Spirit of the Lord stopped talking to him (1 Sam. 28:6). When the Spirit of the Lord stops talking to a soul, the person is left to embrace a reprobate mind.

> Speaking lies in hypocrisy; having their conscience seared with a hot iron...
>
> —1 TIMOTHY 4:2, KJV

PRAYER OF FREEDOM

Lord God, please search my heart and make sure my conscience is not seared. Forgive me for the times and seasons when I ignored You. I repent. Holy Spirit, I surrender my mind to You. Lord Jesus, I ask You to soften my conscience and cause me to be sensitive to the things of God again. Thank You, Lord. (Keep praying in your own words as the Holy Spirit guides you.)

3. Reprobate mind

A reprobate mind is the end result of having a seared conscience. Since that person's ability to distinguish between good and evil has been taken away through the hardness of their heart, they begin to call good evil and evil good. This is a dangerous place to be because it opens you up to potentially blaspheming the Holy Spirit in attributing the works of God to Satan. Have you ever known someone who just seemed not to care nor had any conviction for the evil things they did? It's possible that a reprobate mind was at work.

An example of this is people involved in organized crime. Committing acts of crime comes easy to them, and since the organization is built and sustained by it, such individuals give themselves over to a reprobate mind. A mind that is reprobate can never truly repent for the things they do because they can't distinguish. They might verbally confess their awareness of their actions, but they have no real sense of repentance to actually stop. Even their good acts of kindness are done through evil, sort of like the Robin Hood lifestyle: "Steal from the rich and give to the poor." Stealing is still wrong!

A reprobate mind causes there to be a change in nature where a person's mind goes from fully functional to becoming abominable. Did you ever wonder, for example, why a church's worship leader can commit sinful acts while serving the clergy, with no personal conviction? It's because they have been given over to a reprobate mind.

They profess that they know God; but in works they deny him, being abominable, and disobedient, and unto every good work reprobate.

—Titus 1:16, kjv

Prayer of Freedom

Lord Jesus, forgive me for allowing myself to receive a reprobate mind. I renounce my life of living in sin and ask that the blood of Jesus would cleanse me from wickedness and help me to be committed as a believer, in Jesus' name! (Keep praying in your own words as the Holy Spirit guides you.)

4. Strong delusion

The following verse again affirms what I've been saying throughout this whole book: that when it comes to curses, it's not demons causing them but rather God fighting against a person for refusing to change. When God sends a strong delusion, it's because this person is at the point of no return and will never change. You might ask if such persons exist. Yes they do, and the Book of Revelation says that in the end times many, in their anger toward the things coming on the earth, will still be in defiance toward heaven and not repent. What would make a person not repent can only be explained by what the verse is saying. God won't let them repent because He sent them a strong delusion so they would believe what is *not* true, and ultimately perish.

Never allow yourself to get to this point because there is no coming back.

> And for this cause God shall send them strong delusion, that they should believe a lie.
> —2 THESSALONIANS 2:11, KJV

No prayer of freedom can be offered at this point, as heaven forbids it just as when God told Samuel not to pray for King Saul anymore.

CONCLUDING THOUGHTS

As we close this chapter, I hope you're able to see just how sin evolves and how when generational curses are not dealt with, they can cross over to the next generations and with each passing one increase in strength and cause havoc. Spend some time in prayer and consider everything we covered in this chapter. Allow the Holy Spirit to reveal what's been going on in your bloodline. The Lord Jesus as our great High Priest and Intercessor is available to help you in this area, and the Holy Spirit will also bring clarity to these issues and help you resolve them.

CHAPTER 7

CATEGORIZATION OF INIQUITY AND CURSES

"Now you are *cursed* and banished from the ground, which has swallowed your brother's blood. No longer will the ground yield good crops for you, no matter how hard you work! From now on you will be a homeless wanderer on the earth." Cain replied to the LORD, "My punishment is too great for me to bear!"

—GENESIS 4:11–13

"Listen to me and make up your minds to honor my name," says the LORD of Heaven's Armies, "or I will bring a terrible *curse* against you. I will curse even the blessings you receive. Indeed, I have already cursed them, because you have not taken my warning to heart."

—MALACHI 2:2

THERE IS NOTHING worse than having the Creator of the universe curse you and banish you. He is the source of all life, the source of all strength, the giver of all blessing and favor. To have Him personally curse you must have been an extreme burden to bear. No wonder Cain told Him, "Your punishment is too much for me to bear!" (See Genesis 4:13.) To have your Creator ordain a punishment that is custom-built just for you would have caused anyone to feel completely abandoned.

The story of Cain in Genesis 4 is a perfect example of making the wrong choices and receiving the full weight of those consequences. In this case it was the murder of his brother, Abel. The demands of justice required that level of punishment, but being the first convicted murderer in human history must have been an extremely heavy burden.

There are many ways in which a Christian can become cursed but only one way that opens the door to all of them, and it can be found in one word: *ignorance*. What you don't know can hurt you. Ignorance is not a luxury that Christians can afford. Our future destiny depends on us totally submitting to the Holy Spirit in making sure that no hindrance or stumbling block can thwart or detour it. The Holy Spirit's role is to make sure the believer isn't caught by surprise in the same manner that a person is caught by surprise when the doctor informs them they have cancer. As cancer alters the life of the person once diagnosed, so can generational curses alter the life of a Christian if left unresolved.

Next we will discuss some ways believers can follow the admonition of the apostle Paul when he told the Corinthian church not to be "ignorant of [the devil's] devices" (2 Cor. 2:11, KJV). The New Living Translation version says, "For we are familiar with his evil schemes." So in this chapter we endeavor to help you become more *aware* and *familiar* with the devil's schemes so you can identify what he has been secretly using against you and your family.

SEVEN ABOMINATIONS THE LORD HATES

The following seven things are considered abominations by heaven, and as we mentioned in chapter 5, all abominations produce generational curses. God treats these seven sins as the real *seven deadly sins*! So distasteful are they to Him that He calls them abominable. You might never have connected these seven sins with the power to initiate a curse, but Scripture is clear: they can and will cause a curse to be activated. Let's look closely now.

> There are six things that the LORD hates, seven that are an abomination to him: haughty eyes, a lying tongue, and hands that shed innocent blood, a heart that devises wicked plans, feet that make haste to run to evil, a false witness who breathes out lies, and one who sows discord among brothers.
>
> —PROVERBS 6:16–19, ESV

1. Haughty eyes

The term "haughty eyes" denotes the act of looking down on people. So to have haughty eyes means viewing oneself as better than others. This can be for many reasons, including things such as finances, family pedigree, and education, where one feels better than someone else. The parable of the tax collector and the Pharisee makes the point clear in the prayer the Pharisee prays: "Lord, thank You that I'm not like this tax collector because _____." (See Luke 18:9–14.) You already know his self-righteous prayer.

Having haughty eyes is not necessarily about having eyes that are haughty but rather having a higher perception of oneself over others. This not only goes for individuals but also applies to organizations, families, churches—you name it.

In the Old Testament we find God advising the children of Israel not to act superior over the foreigner living among them. God would judge all Israelites who treated the foreigner with disdain. I think the sin of *racism* can be rooted in this abomination where one race feels superior to others. Whole movements, such as the KKK (Ku Klux Klan), have theologies built on the superiority of the white race over other races. Four hundred years of slavery has resulted in the rise of other movements that perpetuate the same racial superiority, such as Fruit of Islam, Black Hebrew Israelites, Hispanic identity movements, and so on.

It is one thing to have national pride about one's race, country, and identity but quite another when you feel superior to other races, cultures, and nationalities. We find this sin very prevalent in Jesus' time between the Jews and Samaritans. If you're reading this and the Holy Spirit is convicting you of this sin, repent and ask Him to sever any curse that might be working in your life. The following prayer will help.

PRAYER OF FREEDOM

Heavenly Father, please forgive me for having haughty eyes in belittlement of others around me. Lord, forgive me for practicing that which is an

*abomination to You. Set me free, Lord, and reveal
to me any other area where I might not be pleasing You. Holy Spirit, strengthen me to renounce
all forms of haughtiness, arrogance, and pride. If
there is a curse operating in my life or my family, please reveal it. Thank You, Lord Jesus!* (Keep
praying in your own words as the Holy Spirit
guides you.)

2. Lying tongue

This second abomination is bearing false witness about
oneself and is usually directed as intentionally misleading
others. Everyone lies, and some lies can be perceived as lies
and are quickly not believed by the hearers. But then there
are lies that whole cultures and systems are built around.
An example of this is social media—especially among
ministers—where a Christian influencer fabricates the
success of their ministry, thus creating an illusion among
other ministries whereby some sort of influence is given.
But truly their ministry is nothing more than the result of
a lying tongue.

Everyone seems to be on social media. Now, I'm not
saying social media is wrong, but I am saying that a lying
tongue is strong there. Some people even make a living on
lying. Many people lie about themselves when dating a new
person. Many lie on résumés and get hired for jobs they're
not qualified to do. Heaven considers a lying tongue an
abomination because it creates huge disappointment for
those who have been lied to. Living a lie and believing a lie
is dangerous. And the extremity of the lie can potentially

influence the severity of the curse. Pray this prayer and break the power of lying.

PRAYER OF FREEDOM

Lord, forgive me for having a lying tongue and all the harm it may have caused. I repent. Holy Spirit, I humbly ask You to control my tongue and cause me to speak truth in my inwards parts. I plead with the courtroom of heaven to have mercy on me and set me free from any curses a lying tongue may have caused, in Jesus' name. (Keep praying in your own words as the Holy Spirit guides you.)

3. Shedding innocent blood

The shedding of innocent blood goes beyond abortion. Though abortion fits in this sin category and will produce a generational curse (abortion is murder), it goes much further. From Uriah the Hittite, whom David murdered to cover up his sin of adultery with Bathsheba, to Naboth, whom Jezebel had killed in order to take his vineyard for her husband, King Ahab, this abomination is a vile stench in God's nostrils. The murder of Naboth moved heaven so much that God began laying out a plan to kill Jezebel through Elijah. On the day when Ahab went to claim his vineyard for himself, the Lord told him through the prophet Elijah, "Wasn't it enough that you killed Naboth? Must you rob him, too? Because you have done this, dogs will lick your blood at the very place where they licked the blood of Naboth!" (1 Kings 21:19). He prophesied the death of Jezebel too, proclaiming, "Dogs will eat Jezebel's body..." (v. 23).

All throughout history we find the shedding of innocent blood, as far back as Cain and Abel. Cain's sin in shedding his brother's innocent blood caused the Lord to curse Cain. Usually those suffering under this curse will be plagued with bouts of rage, anger, and deep bitterness. When a man commits fornication that leads to pregnancy and then tells his girlfriend to abort the child, he is just as guilty as his pregnant girlfriend. Both parties are guilty of shedding innocent blood, and it will always produce a curse.

In all the countless deliverance sessions we've conducted on women who suffered an abortion, 100 percent of the time there were wounds of guilt, shame, loss, and grief for having killed an innocent life, and almost always there will be a demon manifesting when confronted. If you committed any form of shedding innocent blood, just know you are under a generational curse and need to repent and renounce what you (or your ancestors) have done in this sin and apply the finished work of Christ on the cross. Stand on the Word of God. Finally, pray the following prayer, and let's break this curse.

PRAYER OF FREEDOM

Jesus, I'm too ashamed to look to heaven for my sin of shedding innocent blood. I know I have broken Your heart in this sin. Forgive me; I repent with my whole heart. I humbly ask You to break

*and sever all curses that shedding innocent blood
may have caused in my life and family, in Jesus'
name.* (Keep praying in your own words as the
Holy Spirit guides you.)

4. Wicked plans

This sin takes on a different form, as it means having a
strategic plan in place for some future benefit. Some plans
can take decades to come to fruition. Evil regimes and governments often set plans in order that solely benefit them
in the future. Whole countries are dominated by such
wicked plans. People of authority scheme wicked plans to
keep those under them in bondage. Sometimes employers devise a wicked plan to keep a particular person who
has earned a promotion from getting it—and give the promotion to their friend instead, or to one who bribed them.
Governments may create laws to benefit themselves rather
than the people they were sworn into office to serve. This is
why heaven says in 1 Timothy 2 to pray for those in authority, so we can live peaceable lives. We can't live peaceable
lives if a wicked plan is being carried out.

In family systems, sometimes parents create future
plans for their children without their consent that aren't
for the benefit of the children but for the parent. For example, a low-income parent living on public assistance will
devise a "wicked plan" to cause their children, who are close
to leaving the home for adult life, to never leave so the parent can receive a monthly government aid check. Thus generations of poverty are created.

There are many other examples of the ways wicked

plans are put into effect. Pray and ask the Holy Spirit to reveal any curses where wicked plans have been in effect in your family bloodline, and begin the process of breaking them by praying the following prayer.

PRAYER OF FREEDOM

Holy Spirit, search my heart and reveal to me if there has been any wicked plan that I may not be aware of. And for those I am aware of, please have mercy on my soul and my household for the years of wicked planning and evil we may have caused and all the harm we did. Wash me in the blood of Jesus. Thank You for cleansing me. (Keep praying in your own words as the Holy Spirit guides you.)

5. Running to evil

This particular sin is a bit more isolated, as most people—believers and nonbelievers—aren't running to do evil. The idea of "running" in this text is not actually running to do evil (though there are many cases where men literally run to do evil); it's more about being "quick" to do evil. The Bible says it's a shame for a person to get involved in a matter without first hearing the details of what really happened (Prov. 18:13). Today's society is given over to quickly running to do evil without first investigating. People on social media are quick to heckle, criticize, and defame each other without considering whom it's affecting. If you're a person given over to gossip, are you quick to join others in conversations that aren't pleasing to God? Do you enjoy watching the demise of others around you? Does your family history show this particular pattern of behavior among family members? If so, then your bloodlines could be under a curse.

Heaven requires us to think on things that are lovely, true, and full of virtue and praise (Phil. 4) and to refrain from being quick to run to things that don't please God. But when a person is hasty to run to evil, it's a clear indication that the law of the Lord isn't in their heart and their mindset is not to obey. Running to do evil is a clear indicator they've rejected the Word of God. Let's pray together and break the generational curse over our lives and the lives of our families.

PRAYER OF FREEDOM

> *Lord Jesus, please have mercy on my soul for living a life that was quick to run to evil. Break and sever all generational curses I may have caused. Holy Spirit, I humbly ask that You remove all demons that may be causing havoc in my family. May the blood of Jesus cover my life and my family. Thank You, Lord, for setting me free.* (Keep praying in your own words as the Holy Spirit guides you.)

6. False witness

In Exodus 20:19 and Deuteronomy 5:20, "the word translated as 'false' is a Hebrew word implying intentional falsification or deception. It assumes a deliberate desire to mislead or distort information, presumably for one's own selfish gain or profit."[1]

All false witnessing is a lie, but not all lies are false witnesses in the sense that not all lies affect the reputation of other persons and the judgment of that person in the sight of still other people.

Bearing false witness is a huge sin in the courtroom of heaven. It's abominable! It not only affects the person whom the false witness is against but also affects everyone connected to them. The ripple effects of bearing false witness against someone can outlast a person's lifetime and affect the family members who are still alive. Generations later those connected to the accused can still be dealing with what potentially started as a lie. What comes to mind is the Salem witch trials. Though many of the accused were actual witches and burned at the stake (the punishment for witches at the time), there were innocent among the guilty. Stories of many women accused of being witches who clearly weren't are too numerous to count. Years later the families of the accused were still dealing with the stigma of false witnesses.

Many remote countries today that haven't had the benefit of modern technology and science still suffer under the plague of superstition. They are quick to falsely accuse someone of sorcery or witchcraft, and such persons are exiled from their community; many are stoned and killed. I know I'm using extreme examples to describe false witnessing, but the same holds true in any community concerning persons who falsely accuse people—especially when they don't agree.

I see many in the church committing this act. Many discernment ministers who are more polarized in their understanding of Scripture will falsely accuse another minister of being a "false teacher" simply because they don't agree with a particular view of Scripture. (The very topic of this book, generational curses, hasn't been fully embraced by the church, and many deliverance ministers have been accused of being false teachers.) The videos are endless as many discernment ministers try to expose or discredit such deliverance ministers, and many will even go as far as saying that such ministers aren't true believers.

I believe that many well-meaning believers will fall under the discipline of the Lord due to *false witnessing* concerning ministries they don't understand. When a minister bears false witness against another minister, they open themselves up to a curse—especially when such accusations aren't true. There is a huge difference between defending the faith and defending your view of the faith. Being quick to place someone in the "false teacher" category over nonessentials, then going public to discredit that ministry, displeases the courtroom of heaven. If you feel convicted by the Holy Spirit in this area, pray the following prayer and get free.

PRAYER OF FREEDOM

Holy Spirit, I stand before the heavenly court to admit my guilt in bearing false witness. Forgive

*me for my sin. I'm wholeheartedly sorry. Please
wash me in the blood of Jesus and break every generational curse I may have caused in my bloodline, in Jesus' name!* (Keep praying in your own
words as the Holy Spirit guides you.)

7. Sowing discord

This sin is self-explanatory. I won't spend much time
here because we are all aware just how much heaven hates
discord among brethren. I can't emphasize enough just how
abominable discord is. The Bible says that when brethren
dwell together in unity it causes the commanded blessing to come down. The opposite is the same. When family
members, married couples, churches, businesses, countries,
and so forth have discord among them, the blessing is cut
off! God can't bless what is not united. But woe to the person that causes such discord.

There is no other sin on this list that God hates more
than this one. Why? Discord originated with Satan. Lucifer's rebellion caused a third of the angels of heaven to join
his rebellion, and they were cast out. Discord finds its origin in heaven. So when a believer sows discord, they are
manifesting the character of Satan. They're re-creating the
rebellion that occurred in heaven. God loves unity and dedicated a whole psalm to describing the blessings that occur
when brethren dwell together in unity. Without a doubt
this sin will produce a generational curse, as God hates
discord—and has since the beginning! Let's pray and break
this curse over our lives.

PRAYER OF FREEDOM

Heavenly Father, You desire Your church to be in unity. Forgive me for the times I have sown seeds of division and discord. I'm sorry for my sin, and I repent. Please break all curses I may have caused in my life. Holy Spirit, please reveal to me all times I may have committed this sin of sowing discord so I may renounce and repent. Thank You, Lord Jesus, for Your mercy! In Jesus' name. (Keep praying in your own words as the Holy Spirit guides you.)

While most of the church looks for the obvious sins, few have thought to look at these particular sins that the Bible calls abominations. I believe that most believers are either presently violating one or more of these seven sins or have ignorantly done so in the past. When I happened to stumble across these sins while doing a keyword search on "abominations," it dawned on me that they are rampant in the church.

LEVELS OF DEPRAVITY

Now let's look at the different levels of depravity in human nature and how heaven deals with them in Scripture.

Evil

The word *evil* is more than an action; it's actually a state of being. The Hebrew definition for *evil* (see Strong's H7451, *ra*)[2] would be too long to write here, as it has many facets according to the Jewish mind, but for the sake of this book I will leave it at this:

> Woe to those who call *evil* good, and good evil; who substitute darkness for light and light for darkness; who substitute bitter for sweet and sweet for bitter!
>
> —ISAIAH 5:20

Wicked

Wickedness is defined as "the state of being wicked; a mental disregard for justice, righteousness, truth, honor, virtue; evil in thought and life; depravity; sinfulness; criminality."[3]

> Repent therefore of this thy *wickedness*, and pray God, if perhaps the thought of thine heart may be forgiven thee.
>
> —ACTS 8:22, KJV

Profane

The word *profane* is defined as "not holy because unconsecrated, impure, or defiled: unsanctified; serving to debase or defile what is holy: irreverent; obscene, vulgar."[4]

> By the multitude of thy merchandise they have filled the midst of thee with violence, and thou hast sinned: therefore I will cast thee as *profane* out of the mountain of God: and I will destroy thee, O covering cherub, from the midst of the stones of fire.
>
> —EZEKIEL 28:16, KJV

SPECIAL CURSES AND SINS

Before we go on, let me state emphatically that Christ broke the power of all curses. His substitutionary work on the cross paid the penalty for all sin and curses. Appropriating the redemption found in Jesus can break even the deepest of curses. I felt it necessary to say this because I don't want this book to present a doom-and-gloom narrative for the believer. We are victorious in Christ, and we're seated with Christ in heavenly places. We've been equipped with the Holy Scriptures and the armor of God to be able to withstand all the fiery darts of the wicked one.

Let this reminder serve as a major encouragement as you continue to read this book. The truth contained within these pages is not intended to glorify evil, nor take away the redemptive power of the cross, but rather to admonish you to be more aware of the devil's devices.

The following list of curses isn't absolute or exhaustive but rather an observance from Scripture that can either be true or worth looking into for further revelation.

Perpetual curses (plagues)

A perpetual curse is a judgment from the courtroom of heaven that is deemed irrevocable. What does the word *irrevocable* mean? "Unable to cancel or recall; that which is unalterable or irreversible."[5]

We find many instances in both the Old and New Testaments where the Lord cursed someone or something with an irrevocable curse. When there's an irrevocable curse, it means heaven deems it "unredeemable." When the Lord classifies something as unredeemable—and He is a God of redemption—it means that He finds it detestable or wants to use it to serve as an example.

In the Old Testament, God cursed various nations and wiped them out of existence because of their idolatry. In the New Testament, Jesus cursed a fig tree for not bearing fruit. We see that in such cases the Lord was so resolute that He wouldn't change His mind. When Lucifer and his angels rebelled, Scripture is clear that God cursed him and banished them from heaven (Ezek. 28), and afterward He cursed the serpent in the Garden of Eden. During the time of Elisha, his servant Gehazi received the Babylonian clothing from Namaan the Syrian, even though Elisha had forbidden him to do so. The end result was a perpetual curse of leprosy upon him and his descendants forever. Look at the verse:

> "Because you have done this, you and your descendants will suffer from Naaman's leprosy *forever.*" When Gehazi left the room, he was covered with leprosy; his skin was white as snow.
>
> —2 KINGS 5:27

Gehazi's curse was along the same lines as that of Achan in taking the accursed thing (Josh. 7) in that it caused the courtroom of heaven to declare a perpetual curse upon him and his bloodline. So as we see from Scripture, there is a biblical premise for perpetual curses.

Temporary curses (plagues)

Another type of curse we find in Scripture is the temporary curse. These are judgments released from heaven for bad behavior, sort of like when a child receives a spanking from their parent for disobedience that warrants consequence. Not all forms of discipline from parents are perpetual. No child is put in "time out" forever. But a child may receive a swift spanking from a parent at any moment; however, that parental anger will eventually subside, and the punishment is lifted when the child learns obedience. God treated the children of Israel like a loving Father would in the upcoming verses.

During the time of Korah's rebellion against Moses and Aaron, heaven moved swiftly and sent a curse in the form of a plague that caused all those who joined the rebellion to die. Including Korah and the defectors, exactly 14,700 people died in this instance. It's my personal belief that many historical plagues that have hit humanity for thousands of years have been our Creator's disciplining hand toward His creation for living their lives in disobedience to His laws. Look at the following verse and you will see how our God is a loving God, but also a disciplining Father who desires us to carry out our lives in full obedience.

> And Moses said to Aaron, "Quick, take an incense burner and place burning coals on it from the altar. Lay incense on it, and carry it out among the people to purify them and make them right with the LORD. The LORD's anger is blazing against them—the plague has already

begun." Aaron did as Moses told him and ran out among the people. The plague had already begun to strike down the people, but Aaron burned the incense and purified the people. He stood between the dead and the living, and the plague stopped. But 14,700 people died in that plague, in addition to those who had died in the affair involving Korah. Then because the plague had stopped, Aaron returned to Moses at the entrance of the Tabernacle.

—Numbers 16:46–50

Temporary curses do happen but don't remain forever. Psalm 103:8–9 declares that God will not remain angry forever. Prayer and repentance can cause this curse to be revoked. The scripture above shows that Aaron took the incense—which represents the prayers of the saints—and began walking among the people, and the curse was stopped. It was a shadow of when prayers of intercession are made to mediate between God and the people, just like when an older sibling pleads with the angered parent to withhold discipline from their younger brother or sister. I'm reminded of the many times my Pentecostal grandmother would intervene with my mother in the middle of a spanking, and my mother would stop.

If you're reading this right now, just know prayer is effective and powerful, so never stop praying for your family members and asking heaven to have mercy on them for their disobedience. Trust me, it works and can cause God to slow down His hand of judgment against them for their rebellion. Jesus is our Advocate, and 1 John 1:9 says that if we confess our sins, He is faithful and just to forgive our sins and to cleanse us of all unrighteousness.

Unintentional curses

Unintentional curses happen more times than we think. They are usually done through ignorance and demonstrate just how severely our actions displease the courtroom of heaven. These curses are usually found in the words we speak. The courtroom of heaven is connected to your mouth. Death and life are in the power of your tongue. So it makes sense that this particular curse is probably the most deadly of these three categories because it's committed more times than the others. I'm not trying to instill fear so that we're paranoid about every word that comes out of our mouths, but I am hoping this section will make us more mindful of the things we say that can have serious consequences (even when we didn't mean what we said).

Let's look at the following story of King David and a man named Shimei. David had spent most of his adult life on the run from King Saul. Stories were circulating around Israel concerning this feud between the king and himself. As with any rumors, some stories were exaggerated, and others caused people to pick sides without knowing the full story. In this instance Shimei took King Saul's side, assuming the rumors about David were true, and began innocently cursing David by throwing stones at him, thinking it was the right thing to do in defending King Saul—but in this instance he was wrong. Eventually this act of harshness toward David cost him his life and the life of Solomon.

Just know that ignorance is not an excuse with the courtroom of heaven.

At first David allowed Shimei to curse him without retaliation, as he assumed God was allowing it for some hidden sin in his life that He wanted to deal with. But years later David became aware that he had been innocent in his encounter with Shimei and gave instruction to King Solomon to carry out judgment against him for what he said. Let's read.

SHIMEI CURSES DAVID

> As King David came to Bahurim, a man came out of the village cursing them. It was Shimei son of Gera, from the same clan as Saul's family. He threw stones at the king and the king's officers and all the mighty warriors who surrounded him. "Get out of here, you murderer, you scoundrel!" he shouted at David. "The LORD is paying you back for all the bloodshed in Saul's clan. You stole his throne, and now the LORD has given it to your son Absalom. At last you will taste some of your own medicine, for you are a murderer!"
>
> —2 SAMUEL 16:5–8

I'm sure in the mind of Shimei it was right to say the things he said toward David because David was, in fact, in a feud with King Saul. I don't think Shimei thought that his actions were inherently wrong, as we're all called to defend those whom we serve. I'm assuming David had this in mind and allowed Shimei to curse him.

> Then David said to Abishai and to all his servants,
> "My own son is trying to kill me. Doesn't this rel-
> ative of Saul have even more reason to do so?
> Leave him alone and let him curse, for the LORD
> has told him to do it. And perhaps the LORD will
> see that I am being wronged and will bless me
> because of these curses today." So David and his
> men continued down the road, and Shimei kept
> pace with them on a nearby hillside, cursing and
> throwing stones and dirt at David.
>
> —2 SAMUEL 16:11–13

The sad part of this story is that Shimei's accusations were not founded on truth but on a rumor. Absalom usurped his way to the throne, and it cost him his life.
Years later the facts of Absalom's death were known to the
children of Israel, and it became clear that David was innocent in the rumor. In David's final words to Solomon before
his death he told Solomon to make sure he repaid Shimei
for the evil he caused.

> And remember Shimei son of Gera, the man from
> Bahurim in Benjamin. He cursed me with a ter-
> rible curse as I was fleeing to Mahanaim. When
> he came down to meet me at the Jordan River, I
> swore by the LORD that I would not kill him. But
> that oath does not make him innocent. You are
> a wise man, and you will know how to arrange a
> bloody death for him.
>
> —1 KINGS 2:8–9

Many believers curse themselves unintentionally with half-truths, assumptions, or misinformation. This happens a lot at church when it comes to the congregation and their leadership. Many believers who aren't serving in leadership roles in their local churches can misjudge the actions of a particular leader (sometimes their pastors) and make off-color comments toward them based on their own limited understanding. Immediately these persons experience unnecessary warfare that alters their lives, and yet such issues are misunderstood as common trials. Rather, they are really judgments from heaven because of their careless behavior in how they handled God's anointed servant.

Now, I don't ascribe to the "touch not my anointed" view that has been abused by many who pose as the servants of God, but God does defend His servants who serve Him faithfully, regardless of their obvious flaws. Many times believers unintentionally curse themselves! We are currently living in the days of Shimei where unintentional accusations are the norm (especially on social media), but right now heaven is saying you can break the effect of the unintentional curses by asking the Holy Spirit to reveal any situation where an unintentional curse exists and offering a sincere prayer of repentance to be cleansed from it. If you don't think unintentional sins are real, then read the following verse:

> If one individual commits an *unintentional* sin, the guilty person must bring a one-year-old female goat for a sin offering.
>
> —NUMBERS 15:27

CHAPTER 8

SATAN'S WEAPONS OF MASS DESTRUCTION

T HOUGH I COULD spend all day writing out curse after curse, for this segment I want to get into what I call "Satan's weapons of mass destruction." I call them that because the sins less frequently seen in Scripture are considered the deadliest. Heaven is saying pay attention when it comes to sins that often fly under the radar! Here are the top seven that I believe have caused the most damage throughout human history and within the church today. They are *vanity, envy, gluttony, racism, dishonor, homosexuality,* and *hip-hop culture.* I included this last one here because I haven't seen any other deliverance ministry target this particular genre of music and the far-reaching culture it creates, which is destroying the youth of today.

VANITY

Satan's number one weapon of mass destruction is *vanity.* This was the sin that caused Satan's downfall, not pride. Vanity opened the door to pride, and Satan fell. Now I know that's not what you were expecting to hear because we've been trained to believe it was pride, but Scripture paints a different picture. Before you read the following verse, consider that the Hebrew word for *vanity* (*yahir*) means haughtiness, boastfulness, and conceit.[1]

> Your heart was filled with pride because of *all
> your beauty*. Your wisdom was corrupted by your
> *love of splendor*.
>
> —EZEKIEL 28:17

As you can see, Satan became *vain* in his thinking because God had created him to be the most beautiful being in all His creation. Ezekiel 28 describes in detail just how beautiful Satan was, and it all boiled down to one thing: he became full of himself! The Bible says that his wisdom was corrupted because of his beauty, not his pride. Scripture doesn't say how long it took for Satan to sin, but it does say that over time he became filled with iniquity. (Notice how Ezekiel says "iniquity" and not "sin.")

We already established that iniquity is committing unrepented sin over long periods of time. Satan sinned with vanity, and it gradually contaminated every other area of his being. That's what vanity does to a person; they become so full of themselves that ultimately it consumes them, and they become haughty (which means to belittle and look down on others) and conceited. Once this sin of vanity consumed Lucifer, he looked down on the other angels around him and suggested they join his rebellion. Once they joined him, he began to entertain pride and desired to be worshipped like his Creator, so he launched an assault to dethrone God. We all know how that story ends.

Vanity is the door that leads to pride.

It has only been in recent years that the Holy Spirit showed me the sin of vanity as the *original sin*, and it was a hard pill to swallow because I began to see this sin everywhere. Once I learned that vanity was also the sin that caused Eve to eat the forbidden fruit, it became clear that this sin is a weapon of mass destruction. Look closely at the following verse to see what was really going on in Eve's mind before she ate.

> And when the woman saw that the tree was good
> for food, and that it was *pleasant to the eyes*, and
> a tree to be desired to make one wise, she took of
> the fruit thereof, and did eat, and gave also unto
> her husband with her; and he did eat.
> —GENESIS 3:6, KJV

Before Eve touched that fruit, it was beautiful to the eyes (vanity), and she became enamored with its beauty. (Sound familiar? Hint, hint—Satan's sin.) Once she became hooked, she reached out her hand and ate the fruit.

Vanity opened the door to the original sin.

Nothing has changed since the garden. In this present day and age, vanity is the root cause of 99 percent of our sins. It's everywhere, yet nowhere. Social media is driven by vanity. Platforms such as Facebook aren't even hiding it; look at its name, Facebook, which means, "Look at my face!" Instagram, another platform owned by the same company (Meta) that owns Facebook, is entirely based on photos—and most notably, "selfies."

If I were to ask you when you last heard a sermon on vanity, what would your response be?

- Vanity leads to fornication.

- Vanity leads to greed.

- Vanity leads to envy.

- Vanity leads to pride (and many more sins).

The potential of vanity gripping a person is fierce because vanity has cords that can tie a person down and hold them in bondage, and only the power of the Holy Spirit can break those cords. The Word of God is powerful enough to cut those cords and set the captive free.

> Woe unto them that draw iniquity with *cords of vanity*, and sin as it were with a cart rope.
> —ISAIAH 5:18, KJV

The apostle Paul knew the danger of vanity, and he encouraged the early church not to walk in vanity like those who aren't in covenant with God. Why? Because vanity will produce a curse. Vanity got Lucifer cursed and banished from heaven, and it caused Adam and Eve to be evicted from the garden.

> This I say therefore, and testify in the Lord, that ye henceforth walk not as other Gentiles walk, in the *vanity [futility] of their mind*.
> —EPHESIANS 4:17, KJV

Right now, if you're reading this, ask the Holy Spirit to remove all forms of vanity in your life and break the generational curse.

PRAYER OF FREEDOM

Holy Spirit, I humbly ask You to reveal all forms of vanity in my life so I can repent. I repent of this sin and ask that all generational curses be revoked right now. Help me to walk in the fruit of humility so that I'm not deceived as Satan was. Set me free right now, in Jesus' name!

ENVY

The next weapon of mass destruction is *envy*. The sin of envy has been around since humans started walking the face of the earth. It's what caused Cain to kill his brother. Murder wasn't what drove Cain to kill Abel; it was envy! The Bible says that envy is more powerful than anger and wrath.

> Wrath is cruel, anger is overwhelming, but who can stand before jealousy [*envy*]?
> —PROVERBS 27:4

Envy is the driving force behind why many people in modern society do the things they do, because they desire to appear better than their peers. The church is no different. Many churches, ministries, and individual believers make it their priority to keep up with the appearances of their brethren. The overdressing on Sunday (nothing wrong with dressing up on Sunday), the flashy cars (nothing wrong with having a nice car), the ministries competing to see who has the largest crowd—envy is rampant in the church! It's rampant in families, it's rampant in business and trade, it's rampant in government. Envy is everywhere. For a lot of people, "living the good life" is not driven by a desire to enjoy their quality of life. No, it's to appear better than their peers. Social media is riddled with selfies of people enjoying life to show the world just how good they're doing "living," but the real motivation is to keep up with the Joneses.

> And I saw that all toil and all achievement spring
> from one person's *envy* of another. This too is
> meaningless, a chasing after the wind.
> —ECCLESIASTES 4:4, NIV

What people fail to realize is that envy has the potential to poison your body. It's not just a sin of the heart but also of the body. The Bible says that envy can rot the bones!

> A heart at peace gives life to the body, but *envy*
> rots the bones.
> —PROVERBS 14:30, NIV

One thing we know for sure is that envy is what took Jesus to the cross. Envy is what caused the Pharisees, Sadducees, and teachers of the Law to despise Jesus' earthly ministry. When I first started studying this sin, it was an eye-opener to me because before that I'd always assumed the religious leaders hated Jesus. The text doesn't say they hated Him; it says they *envied* Him.

Envy can poison your spiritual senses and cause you not to see clearly to the point that you would actually betray the Son of God. Pontius Pilate discerned very quickly that Jesus was innocent of breaking any law, and he was determined to release Him. The Sanhedrin's persistence in wanting Jesus convicted as a criminal made it clear to Pilate that *envy* was driving them. This sin of envy is also part of the Ten Commandments (Deut. 5:21), where God says, "Do not covet what your neighbor has" (paraphrased).

> As the crowds gathered before Pilate's house that morning, he asked them, "Which one do you want me to release to you—Barabbas, or Jesus who is called the Messiah?" (He knew very well that the religious leaders had arrested Jesus out of *envy*.)
>
> —MATTHEW 27:17–18

Today as you read this, you can be set free from envy. The Holy Spirit is here to set the captives free. Don't allow envy to contaminate what God is doing in your life. Don't open the door to that curse! It caused Cain to fall, it caused the Pharisees to stumble, and the Bible says that it can also poison your body. Cut it out right now by praying the following prayer.

PRAYER OF FREEDOM

Lord Jesus, forgive me of envy and being jealous of others. It's poisoning my life and my family. I repent of my sin of envy! Holy Spirit, please break all generational curses that were activated in my

*life and my household through envy. I'm humbly
asking now, in Jesus' name!*

GLUTTONY

The Hebrew word for *gluttony* (*zolel*) means "to shake out"
or "to squander."[2] The idea is to be a waster by always
feeling you don't have enough. Gluttony is about having
unrestrained desire, or desires that aren't under control.
Gluttony is about more than food. Though food is part
of it, it's really the idea of never being satisfied or content.
Today's society is dominated by never having enough. Con-
sumerism is America's greatest flaw. Americans consume
more than they give. The political battles we see on television concerning America are all centered on trade, import,
and export. Why? Because as a nation we are gluttonous!
The God of the Bible is no longer the God of this country;
instead we worship the god of the belly.

> Whose end is destruction, whose God is their
> *belly*, and whose glory is in their shame, who
> mind earthly things.
>
> —PHILIPPIANS 3:19, KJV

Gluttony actually has the potential to replace God in
the minds of people. Gluttony can become a false god, causing people to erect false ideologies in their minds around
it. Whole countries are dominated by gluttony while others die of starvation. Gluttony was the sin that caused God
to judge Sodom and Gomorrah. I know we've been taught

that homosexuality was the sin that caused their destruction, but according to Ezekiel it was gluttony.

> Sodom's sins were pride, *gluttony*, and laziness, while the poor and needy suffered outside her door.
>
> —EZEKIEL 16:49

Heaven judged the cities of Sodom and Gomorrah harshly because of gluttony, and this sin will always produce a generational curse. (See Numbers 11:31–34.) God places gluttony in the category of *iniquity*, making it extremely dangerous. The vast majority of our country is overweight, and obesity produces unproductive citizens, as their obesity causes many to stay home and embrace a lifestyle of laziness that doesn't contribute to the workforce. Also, what Paul said regarding "anyone who doesn't work, doesn't eat" now makes it clear why one of the fruits of the Spirit is *self-control*.

> Therefore in that day the Lord GOD of hosts called you to weeping, to wailing, to shaving the head and to wearing sackcloth. Instead, there is gaiety and gladness, killing of cattle and slaughtering of sheep, *eating* of meat and drinking of wine: "Let us eat and drink, for tomorrow we may die." But the LORD of hosts revealed Himself to me, "Surely this iniquity shall not be forgiven you until you die," says the Lord GOD of hosts.
>
> —ISAIAH 22:12–14, NASB95

As you can see from this verse, a generational curse can be activated upon households if gluttony has replaced a good work ethic. During the Israelites' journey in the wilderness, they complained against Moses and Aaron by saying, "You brought us to the wilderness to die," and, "It would have been better to die in Egypt, for at least we had meat to eat." (See Exodus 16:3.) The Lord was so angered by their murmuring that He caused a severe plague to wipe out the complainers, and He used them as a lesson for all to see that gluttony will not be tolerated. Many Israelites died that day and were buried, and the name of the place was called "graves of gluttony."

> But while they were gorging themselves on the meat—while it was still in their mouths—the anger of the LORD blazed against the people, and he struck them with a severe plague. So that place was called Kibrothhattaavah (which means "graves of *gluttony*") because there they buried the people who had craved meat from Egypt.
>
> —NUMBERS 11:33–34

Pray this prayer right now, and break free from the curse of gluttony.

PRAYER OF FREEDOM

Heavenly Father, forgive me for the sin of gluttony and making my desires more important than Your perfect will. I repent! Lord Jesus, set me free and break every generational curse I have

*activated through gluttony. Holy Spirit, cause me
to walk in the fruit of self-control, in Jesus' name.*

RACISM

And Miriam and Aaron spake against Moses
because of the Ethiopian woman whom he had
married: for he had married an Ethiopian woman.
—NUMBERS 12:1, KJV

You're probably saying to yourself, What does racism have
to do with generational curses? Everything! Racism is a
learned behavior that is passed down from generation to
generation. It's not something new within the last five hundred years but has been around since Bible times, and God
has plenty to say about it. Yes, racism will produce a generational curse.

What is racism? Racism can be defined as "prejudice,
discrimination, or antagonism by an individual, community, or institution against a person or people on the basis
of their membership in a particular racial or ethnic group,
typically one that is a minority or marginalized."[3]

The opening verse remains the most outspoken Scripture text concerning potential racism. I'm not saying Miriam and Aaron were racists, but it's very clear they were
bothered that Moses married a black woman (Cushite =
Ethiopian), a woman of color who wasn't in covenant with
the God of the Hebrews. It makes sense that Moses would
marry a black woman, as he was raised in Egypt (in Africa).

Let's look more closely at another portion of Scripture
where it's obvious that racism is being described in the text.

The Bible says that King David was white-skinned and ruddy (1 Sam. 16:12), so it makes sense that his son King Solomon would also be of lighter complexion and ruddy (reddish).

> My beloved is white and ruddy, the chiefest among ten thousand.
> —SONG OF SOLOMON 5:10, KJV

So we see this verse describing, in the words of Solomon's beloved, just how fair-looking he was among all the other men in Israel, as he resembled his father, David. Not only was he handsome like his father, but he also had the same sexual issues that his father had. (We dealt with this in more detail in chapter 6.) Solomon ended up marrying a woman of Egypt—Pharaoh's daughter—and this story can be found in 1 Kings 11:1–10, where we see that after Solomon built the temple in Jerusalem, he also built Pharaoh's daughter a house. This marriage was designed to make a peace alliance between Egypt and Israel, but Solomon really did love her, and the Hebrew women hated it! Not only were they filled with jealousy—it was every Hebrew girl's wish to be married to the king—but now their hopes were dashed by this outsider, and because she was of darker skin, they forced her to work the fields.

> I am black, but comely, O ye daughters of Jerusalem, as the tents of Kedar, as the curtains of Solomon. Look not upon me, because I am black, because the sun hath looked upon me: my mother's children were angry with me; they

made me the keeper of the vineyards; but mine
own vineyard have I not kept.

—SONG OF SOLOMON 1:5–6, KJV

This verse is very clear: they hated her because she was
black, and history has shown through the transatlantic
slave trade of African Americans that this same hatred still
exists in modern times, sometimes in the church. Those of
darker skin have been forced to work the fields (the text
says "vineyards"). Regardless of where it exists, racism still
produces a generational curse. Many groups such as the Ku
Klux Klan and other racial hate groups claim Christianity
as their religion and pride themselves in the separation of
the races—they even use Scripture to justify these actions.
The Bible is clear that in Christ there is neither bond nor
free, neither Jew nor Gentile. Christ came to break the
middle wall of separation.

> There is neither Jew nor Gentile, neither slave nor
> free, nor is there male and female, for you are all
> one in Christ Jesus.
>
> —GALATIANS 3:28, NIV

When a person claims to profess Christ but still holds on
to the belief in the separation of the races and treats their
fellow peers of different races with contempt, they open
themselves to a generational curse. Ask the Holy Spirit to
show you where you might have been partial in your view
toward someone of a different race. If God reveals to you
that your family is indeed racist, pray the following prayer
below and get set free.

PRAYER OF FREEDOM

Heavenly Father, forgive me and my bloodline for racism. Forgive me for treating those outside my race as inferior. Holy Spirit, please regenerate my mind from racism in all forms, and set me free from every curse. Lord Jesus, my family bloodline is racist, but I plead at the mercy of the courtroom of heaven and ask that You set me free. I repent for every instance where I treated with contempt anyone outside of my race. Break the curse! I now declare that all races are made in Your image and likeness and are worthy of dignity, respect, and honor.

DISHONOR

"Listen to me and make up your minds to *honor* my name," says the LORD of Heaven's Armies, "or I will bring a terrible curse against you. I will curse even the blessings you receive. Indeed, I have already cursed them, because you have not taken my warning to heart."

—MALACHI 2:2

To me, this particular curse sticks out more than any other curse in recent times. Because we're living in a fatherless generation, we are witnessing the byproduct of a people who have *no honor* or respect for anyone. Children don't honor parents, citizens don't honor government officials, employees don't honor their employers, and church members don't even honor their pastors. The list of dishonor is endless.

There was a time when honor was prevalent in our culture, but with the passing of each generation we see honor depleting more and more. The culture of the internet is saturated with dishonor. It's everywhere and very prevalent in the church.

What is dishonor? According to biblehub.com it means "lack of honor; disgrace; ignominy; shame; reproach."[4]

Heaven is so serious about dishonor that to commit it was considered a capital offense, punishable by death.

> Anyone who *dishonors* father or mother must be put to death. Such a person is guilty of a capital offense.
>
> —LEVITICUS 20:9

Today, at least in the West, no one is going to be executed because of dishonor, but in other countries such as North Korea, Turkmenistan, and some Middle Eastern countries it is punishable by death to dishonor one's own country's leader or the country itself.

I believe the same capital punishment exists for us in the West, only it's in the spirit. I've seen countless Christians walk in the same sin as Reuben in the Bible and receive the same judgment. Reuben dishonored his father, Jacob, and lost his birthright.

> The oldest son of Israel was Reuben. But since he *dishonored* his father by sleeping with one of

> his father's concubines, his birthright was given
> to the sons of his brother Joseph. For this reason,
> Reuben is not listed in the genealogical records as
> the firstborn son.
>
> —1 CHRONICLES 5:1

The youngest son of Noah (Ham) also dishonored his father by telling his brothers about Noah's drunkenness and nakedness, and when Noah woke up, he cursed Ham's firstborn because of Ham's dishonor. In rebuking the Pharisees for not obeying the commandment of honoring their parents, Jesus said they were on dangerous territory in not fulfilling that commandment. (See Matthew 15:6.)

The commandment of honoring your parents and people of authority is found all over the Old Testament (Exod. 22:22), and it was punishable by death or extreme judgment.

How many believers violate this commandment more than any other is yet to be determined, but I have seen numerous believers dishonor their church leadership without realizing that the hardship they currently face or dealt with in the past is the direct judgment because of it. Even if you told them they wouldn't believe it, because modern evangelicalism has explained away such Bible verses as "touch not my anointed" (Ps. 105:15, ESV). I'm aware that many leaders abuse their power and authority by quoting that verse when being held accountable for bad behavior; I'm not referring to that group of charlatans. But I am referring to those who walk in true holiness and are dishonored by some immature believers. I have seen many cases where such persons are constantly in hardship and can't make the connection that their conflict is the result of walking in dishonor.

If you're reading this, be careful of what you post online on various social media platforms. These platforms reek of dishonor, as everyone is trying to be right and appear smart. I have even seen well-meaning Christians debate on social media or shame other believers they disagree with. I've seen young believers dishonor pastors and leaders on Facebook, TikTok, and other platforms over minor disagreements, not realizing moments like that can open their lives to a generational curse.

A family who once attended our church lived in a constant state of negative drama, and I personally came to their aid both in prayer and in material ways many times. One common denominator I observed was that they would often dishonor church leadership, then repent to me for gossiping or misunderstanding my vision for the church. Eventually they left the church, and now years later whenever I see this family, they're still in the same condition and still dishonoring the church.

If you can identify with the family I just described, if you have issues with dishonor and are now making the connection that you've been suffering from the curse of dishonor, I urge you to pray the following prayer, and watch God break the curse and set you free!

PRAYER OF FREEDOM

Heavenly Father, forgive me and my bloodline for dishonor. I repent, and I repent for my bloodline!

> *May the courtroom of heaven declare me and*
> *my bloodline free from the curses that were ini-*
> *tiated because of dishonor. Forgive me for dis-*
> *honoring* _____ *(say the names the*
> *Holy Spirit reveals). I renounce every demon*
> *that came into my life because of dishonor, and*
> *I order them to go now in Jesus' name. Lord Jesus,*
> *I receive Your freedom from the curse of dishonor*
> *now, in Your name!*

HOMOSEXUALITY

If a man practices *homosexuality*, having sex with
another man as with a woman, both men have
committed a detestable act. They must both
be put to death, for they are guilty of a capital
offense.

—LEVITICUS 20:13

Do not practice *homosexuality*, having sex with
another man as with a woman. It is a detestable
sin.

—LEVITICUS 18:22

There is no way around these verses. While modern civilization calls them antiquated, the Holy Bible is very clear:
homosexuality, along with other inordinate sexual desires
such as bestiality and incest, are not just regular sins but
are condemned as abominations. This doesn't mean homosexual people are abominable, but the act of homosexuality is. In all instances in Scripture where such sins are

mentioned, there's never a moment where this is a gray area, where maybe it was permissible or understood through genetics. No! All who practiced homosexuality in the Old Testament were met with extreme judgment.

Homosexuality is a sin and produces a generational curse. Look at the following verse in the New Testament and you will see that God hasn't changed His mind, as He wanted the apostle Jude to remind the readers. (Jude was one of Mary's sons, a half-brother to Jesus.)

> Even as Sodom and Gomorrah, and the cities about them in like manner, giving themselves over to fornication, and going after strange flesh, are set forth for an example, suffering the vengeance of eternal fire.
>
> —JUDE 7, KJV

You may be asking, Why would God be so draconian toward same-sex attraction when He's given mankind the blessing of free will? The answer is simple: It goes against God's original mandate for mankind and the earth. The command was to be fruitful and multiply.

> Then God blessed them and said, "Be fruitful and multiply. Fill the earth and govern it. Reign over the fish in the sea, the birds in the sky, and all the animals that scurry along the ground."
>
> —GENESIS 1:28

As you can see, the command wasn't just to be fruitful; the verse also says, "Fill the earth." The Book of Isaiah gives more detail about the earth's mandate, when God said that He desires for the earth "to be inhabited." Anything less would mean He created the earth in vain, which is why *not* fulfilling this commandment causes severe consequences.

> For thus saith the LORD that created the heavens; God himself that formed the earth and made it; he hath established it, he created it not in vain, he formed it to be inhabited: I am the LORD; and there is none else.
>
> —ISAIAH 45:18, KJV

What does Genesis 1:28 have to do with homosexuality/lesbianism? The issue is not love. Two men in love with each other can live fruitful lives, but they can't reproduce! Two men or two women can never multiply. Mankind could not survive more than a generation if everyone on earth became homosexual/lesbian and abandoned their love for the opposite sex. The issue is reproduction, not love. The courtroom of heaven takes such sins seriously.

There are a lot of other reasons why God holds this sin as one of the abominations in producing a generational curse, but let me say this to all who read this: *you don't have to agree with me concerning homosexuality*. I know that this present cancel culture and LGBTQ+ agenda is hard at work trying to change the biblical narrative, but it still doesn't change God's Word! Please don't shoot the messenger for remaining faithful to the message. I'm not trying to be judgmental toward homosexuals, nor am I trying to paint a picture of a doom-and-gloom gospel, but I *am* trying to show you the need to speak the Prayer of Freedom below and break the generational curse.

If you are reading this and you're openly gay or secretly struggling with same-sex attraction, I just want you to know that Jesus came to set the captives free. You will have a long road ahead of you in recovering and changing your lifestyle, but at least you can begin that journey knowing the curse has been broken.

PRAYER OF FREEDOM

Heavenly Father, I realize that same-sex attraction is a sin before the courtroom of heaven. I repent for my sins in this area and ask that the blood of Jesus be applied to break all curses of sexual confusion and gender-identity sins. I ask that You clean my bloodline from this sin. Lord Jesus, remove all demons that have been given legal access to me and my family. Holy Spirit, I ask You to regenerate my mind and soul and restore my true identity, in Jesus' name!

HIP-HOP CULTURE

This particular sin is different, and I wanted to include it in my list of "weapons of mass destruction" because I haven't seen anyone else address it or even attempt to confront it. Now, I know for many of you reading this book, hip-hop is not a style of music you're into, but I mention it because if you have children, they are likely into hip-hop culture.

Hip-hop as a cultural movement attained widespread popularity in the 1980s and '90s. It is also the backing music for rap, the musical style incorporating rhythmic and/or rhyming speech that became the movement's most lasting and influential art form.

Let me start by saying hip-hop culture is not sinful, but its ideologies and philosophies are 100 percent sinful! For me to say that hip-hop culture is sinful, I would also have to include all forms of music such as rock, country, opera, and so on, as they have their issues as well. I mention hip-hop because no other musical genre is so connected to controlling the way people think and live.

Right now, hip-hop is the only musical genre that is universally accepted in every sector of society. No other genre has been able to do that. Hip-hop is everywhere. From commercials on television to movies to sporting events to government rallies that use rappers in their campaigns, almost all professionals and every profession uses hip-hop. Many gang members use hip-hop to play in their cars while they go to commit crimes. I recently saw a TV meteorologist dancing hip-hop in a video on TikTok. I myself come from hip-hop culture, and I can tell you that the music heavily influenced a lot of the evil I did.

Why is hip-hop so attractive? It can't just be the music. What causes those who listen to the music to want to go and live the lifestyle of its songs? I don't agree with those who say the music controls them, but I do believe the music *influences* them. At its core, hip-hop is built on the values of social justice, peace, respect, self-worth, community, and having fun. But those core values have been replaced by a new set of values: social justice has been replaced by rebellion against government, peace has been replaced by hostility toward peers (a.k.a. competition), respecting your peers has been replaced with disrespect, self-worth has been replaced with devaluing others (especially women), community has been replaced with murder, and having fun has been replaced with money.

These new values fill the music's lyrics and have caused the culture to be filled with *curses* and many people to become enslaved. Some are so enslaved by this hip-hop lifestyle that they can't function without it. Many people are so devoid of self-worth that their hearts are filled with murder, they don't value relationships, and money is the driving force of everything they do. (This is why flashing money is dominant in hip-hop pictures and videos.)

Our youth are depressed, isolated, on the brink of suicide, and can't function in society, so they live in communities huddled around this music. Thank God that heaven loves them and has saved many of them and sent them back as hip-hop evangelists using Christian rap to reach their peers. But it's not enough, and many Christian rappers are overlooked by the church and have no support from the body of Christ at large. The church needs to come alongside these hip-hop ministers and evangelists and surround them with accountability and biblical discipline so the sins and curses that dominate secular hip-hop don't grip them as well. Now you know why I thought it necessary to mention this culture. If you're reading this right now, you can be free. Let me give you an example of a deliverance session in which demons of hip-hop manifested and were ultimately defeated by the power of Jesus' name.

DELIVERED FROM THE CURSE
OF HIP-HOP CULTURE

One day I was approached by a close friend of mine who is an apostle of a thriving church in New Jersey. He asked if I would take him through deliverance, as he was sensing heaven telling him that he needed it. I agreed to see him, and when he came to my office, I began to take him through deliverance. Midway through the session, I sensed the need to call out the demons of hip-hop (this was actually my first time doing that), and as soon as I called them out, my friend gave a loud, prolonged yell that lasted fifteen to twenty seconds. While he was yelling, the demons manifested, and I said firmly, "Curse of hip-hop culture, come out!" Then I said, "Curse of the orphan spirit, come out!" Finally I said, "Every demon that came into his life through hip-hop culture, come out!" The next two minutes were ugly as the demons manifested, and one by one they came out.

If I could use a Scripture passage to describe what hip-hop culture is doing to people and how it's opening the door to a curse, it would be the story of Elisha and the forty-two youths. One day the prophet Elisha was traveling and came across a group of youths who became disrespectful. The text doesn't say what type of upbringing these boys had, but I'm sure there are similarities among youth groups all over the world during any era. Youth that haven't been raised in loving homes, with father figures present, will suffer the need for affirmation and acceptance and will find it with other disenfranchised youth.

The following text describes what we would call in the street a "posse" or "gang." The text doesn't say that, but why would forty-two youths be traveling together? Youth not raised to respect older people or people of esteemed rank will dishonor and disrespect them. Such was the case with Elisha. They disrespected the prophet, the man of God. Their making fun of his bald head ultimately led to the prophet decreeing a curse over them.

Ironically, this story depicts what is happening to those enslaved to hip-hop culture. Let's read together.

> Elisha left Jericho and went up to Bethel. As he was walking along the road, a group of boys from the town began mocking and making fun of him. "Go away, baldy!" they chanted. "Go away, baldy!" Elisha turned around and looked at them, and he cursed them in the name of the LORD. Then two bears came out of the woods and mauled forty-two of them.
>
> —2 KINGS 2:23–24

PRAYER OF FREEDOM

Lord Jesus, forgive me for being enslaved to hip-hop culture. Forgive me for having hip-hop as an idol in my life. I repent for allowing hip-hop to control my way of thinking, my way of living, and my way of being. I renounce hip-hop culture's evil

THE SECRETS TO GENERATIONAL CURSES

> ideologies that strayed from its original purpose.
> Heavenly Father, please break all forms of gener-
> ational curses that have been activated in my life
> through this genre of music. From today forward
> I will listen to music that is both godly and edify-
> ing, in Jesus' name!

CONCLUDING THOUGHTS

The last few chapters weren't fun, but they were informa-
tive and necessary—a crash course in learning as much as
you can and allowing the Holy Spirit to recalibrate your
thinking so you're more aware of Satan's devices. Ask the
Holy Spirit to enlarge your capacity to receive understanding. Ask Him to embed everything you've learned into
your spirit so that when the time comes to discern the root
causes of curses in your life, or in the lives of others, you
will be sharp and accurate.

CHAPTER 9

PRAYERS TO REMOVE DEEP CURSES

"Now you are *cursed and banished* from the ground, which has swallowed your brother's blood. No longer will the ground yield good crops for you, no matter how hard you work! From now on you will be a homeless wanderer on the earth." Cain replied to the LORD, "My punishment is too great for me to bear!"

—GENESIS 4:11–13

You have come to Jesus, the one who mediates the new covenant between God and people, and to the sprinkled blood, which speaks of forgiveness instead of *crying out for vengeance* like the blood of Abel.

—HEBREWS 12:24

Then the Lord said, "Learn a lesson from this unjust judge. Even he rendered a just decision in the end. So don't you think God will surely give justice to his chosen people who cry out to him day and night? Will he keep putting them off? I tell you, he will grant justice to them quickly! But when the Son of Man returns, *how many will he find on the earth who have faith?*"

—LUKE 18:6–8

SATAN IS A legalist. He's confined to the regulations and stipulations of the courtroom of heaven. So *if you find the right law*, then Satan and the curse have to release you. You need to understand this principle, which was clearly seen in the Book of Job. Satan couldn't attack Job unless the courtroom of heaven allowed it. In this chapter I'm hoping you will learn that the most effective method for winning spiritual warfare is to fight the devil legally. This is why Jesus used the Scriptures when contending with the devil during His forty days of temptation. Scripture is the constitution of heaven, and when we quote it in proper context, we are reciting heaven's laws, which have been given to protect us as citizens of the kingdom of God.

This chapter will provide insight into how you can take legal action against the enemy through Scripture and see immediate results—or at least start the process of winning your case in the courtroom of heaven.

HEAVEN'S DESIRE FOR BLOODLINES

God's greatest desire is for human beings to enjoy fellowship with Him and with one another. God didn't create us for destruction or misery; He created us to be fruitful, multiply, and have dominion. Heaven's original intent for humanity was "blessing," which is why you find many times in the beginning of creation (Genesis) the phrase "and God blessed them." Even when He destroyed the world through the flood, immediately upon Noah and his family leaving the ark, we see God blessing them again, letting us know that no matter how much humans veer off, His lovingkindness toward us will never waver.

This is cause for great rejoicing. If you're reading this and feel like you've committed unpardonable sin or come from a family that doesn't have God as the focus of their lives, just know that heaven allowed you to read this book because it's not too late to start anew in Christ and live a victorious Christian life. Right now you can get free and stay free by applying the principles in this chapter, but your perspective has to change from "God is against me" to "God is for me." Nothing is more frustrating than when people misunderstand your intention and heart. God is the same way. Most families raise their children with a distorted view of God and assume He is out to get them, but such is not the case.

Centuries after God mandated Noah and his sons to repopulate the earth, we find God calling a man named Abram. He and his family were called by God to leave their original homeland and travel to a new one, where heaven was going to birth a nation that would be exclusively selected to be His priests. But He started by saying to Abram, "In you all the families of the earth shall be blessed" (Gen. 12:3, ESV). God is always thinking about blessing families, not destroying them. God's intention for families hasn't changed, and because of Jesus' work of redemption on the cross, His mercy can now extend for multiple generations. In fact, Scripture says that His blessing can reach even as far as a thousand generations of those who love Him (Exod. 20:6). The following verse also expresses this point.

> The counsel of the LORD stands forever, the thoughts and plans of His heart through all generations.
>
> —PSALM 33:11, AMP

God's love is being extended right now as you read this. Allow this verse to shift the narrative of how you view God. He's not out to destroy you but to restore you and help you and your family break the curses in your lives!

> You have forgiven the wickedness of Your people; You have covered all their sin. Selah. You have withdrawn all Your wrath, You have turned away from Your burning anger.
>
> —PSALM 85:2–3, AMP

How does one begin the process of breaking a generational curse? It's not through praying some "vain repetition" prayer that Jesus condemned in Matthew 6 concerning those who don't know Him, but rather a focused prayer that targets where the curse might be rooted and then uprooting it in Jesus' name!

Although when Jesus breaks the curse it will be swift and instantaneous, the process of getting there requires some soul-searching. (I'm not referring to a works-based gospel or legalism.) Generations of rebellion in our bloodline must be dealt with just like a real legal case. Some legal cases are quick, and the cases are thrown out of court, while others are long and dragged out. We find this with the Amorites, when God told Abraham, "For the iniquity of the Amorites is not yet complete" (Gen. 15:16, ESV). Centuries later God tells Moses to instruct the children of Israel to wipe out the Amorites. What I'm trying to show you is that when God deals with nations, as well as people, it might take years and possibly centuries for His case against them to come up before Him.

There's no quick "bandage" solution for breaking a curse, but these prayers that you've prayed so far are the beginning of heaven starting your trial case in the heavenly court. As you continue to read this book and pray the prayers, by the time you reach the end of the book, you will be completely free! Christ made it possible through His redemptive work.

Again, the moment of freedom is instant, but getting to that moment will take some time. Even Daniel had to tarry for twenty-one days to get an answer. I'm not saying you will have to wait twenty-one days, but I am saying it will require some time for heaven to see just how serious you are about resolving the issues in your life and bloodline. I believe this is why in the Gospels the Lord gave us the parable about the unjust judge. Though the parable is about prayer, it still shows the parallel between the earthly courtroom and the courtroom of heaven. Let's look closely at the parable and glean what we can from it.

INTERCESSORY PRAYER (LUKE 18:1–8)

This parable is by far the most encouraging when it comes to understanding how the courtroom of heaven operates.

"There was a judge in a certain city" (v. 2).

The text opens by saying there was a judge in a certain city. This is already telling us not to view things from a relationship narrative but from a legal one! The text doesn't say, "There was a father." This small detail is important because most Christians view their Christian experience only from the lens of relationship. This parable immediately lets us know that it should be read from a legal worldview, not a relational one.

"...who neither feared God nor cared about people" (v. 2).

Next the parable says that the judge was impartial, meaning he didn't fear God or man. This allows us to see into the character of the judge—he didn't accept bribes and always dealt fairly when it came to justice.

"A widow of that city came to him repeatedly, saying, 'Give me justice in this dispute with my enemy'" (v. 3).

The story tells us there was a widow, and we learn that she had experienced some loss. The text doesn't say how she lost her husband, but it does say that she was seeking justice—meaning she had been wronged or there was some sort of legal wrong. You don't demand justice unless your legal rights have been violated. Her rights had been violated by an enemy. This is a picture of our battle against the enemy of our soul! This woman had gotten into a dispute with her enemy, and apparently couldn't prevail over her enemy, so she went to seek justice from a higher authority. This happens many times with believers who try to live victoriously against the enemy but are thwarted.

"The *judge ignored her for a while*, but finally he said to himself, 'I don't fear God or care about people'" (v. 4).

From here the text says that for "a while" the judge wouldn't give her justice. At this point most people—believers included—can identify. Throughout the years we pray and pray and pray and wonder why there hasn't been a change. We make some slight changes in our behavior by praying more, fasting more, and reading the Word more, yet there seems to be some unspoken defeat that still affects the believer. I've seen many believers endure years of defeat, and no matter how much you encourage them to live victoriously in Christ through Scripture, they still end up defeated. The parable doesn't say how long the judge ignored her request, but we know heaven is trying to show us that it can be long years of waiting for change.

From this point on the parable takes a drastic turn. The widow goes from years of no answer from the judge to an immediate answer, and this shows a hidden truth about how to begin the process of resolving a generational curse. As I mentioned before, there wasn't a quick bandage solution for the widow, nor a quick "fix-it" prayer—it required two elements: *time* and *persistence*.

If you're going to resolve any or all generational curses in your life, it's going to require time: time spent with God, seeking Him and asking Him for clarity on why you sense that you might have a generational curse. Going to court is never a quick event. It takes time to stand in line waiting to enter the courtroom, then finding the right department that addresses your complaint, then filing the complaint, and so on.

I'm not trying to make this process difficult, because

we have been given access to "come boldly to the throne of grace" (Heb. 4:16, NKJV). But I also don't want anyone to think it's so easy. The parable lets us know it's going to take some work on the part of the believer as they seek for justice from heaven on their behalf.

I want to encourage every reader as you work through the rest of this book—and as you spend time with God in fasting and prayer and bombard the throne of grace with pleas, like the widow did—to ask God to reveal what curses could be hindering your Christian walk.

The parable has a happy ending; the judge declares, "I'm going to see that she gets justice" (Luke 18:5), and brings her swift justice. Be encouraged; God has already begun the process of breaking the generational curses affecting your life. Your case is about to be resolved.

PRAYERS TO HELP YOU WIN IN THE COURTROOM OF HEAVEN

Understanding the different types of prayers is crucial to winning this battle against the kingdom of darkness in the courtroom room of heaven. Knowing the difference will help you in *binding* and *loosing*. But not all prayer is the same, just as all language in the courtroom isn't the same. The reason we hire a lawyer is because (1) we don't know the *law*, and (2) we don't know the *language* of the courtroom. Winning and losing cases comes down to these two things. If a lawyer knows the law, he or she will be able to communicate and potentially win the case.

Most Christians haven't been taught the different

categories of prayer and, sadly, are defeated. For example, confronting a generational curse is done not through prayer but through pleading, just as healing a sickness is done not through pleading but through prayer. The Book of James says, "Is anyone among you sick? Let them call the elders of the church to *pray* over them and anoint them with oil in the name of the Lord" (5:14, NIV). Notice the text doesn't say, "Let them plead over them with oil." No need to plead when all that is required is to pray!

Look at the following verse, and you will see praying and pleading are not the same. As Jesus went around doing good and healing all who were oppressed by the devil, many of those battles were won either through prayer or pleading!

> While Jesus was here on earth, he offered *prayers* and *pleadings*, with a loud cry and tears, to the one who could rescue him from death. And God heard his prayers because of his deep reverence for God.
> —HEBREWS 5:7

We see from the text that Jesus knew when to *pray* and ask His heavenly Father, and when to *plead* and pull on the heavenly court. The same is needed to appropriate what Jesus did on the cross to break all generational curses. Take a few moments and learn the difference here.

Pleading (Isa. 64:7)
Pleading—"a formal statement of the cause of an action or defense"[1]

Supplication (Acts 1:14, NKJV)

Supplication—"the action of asking or begging for something earnestly or humbly"[2]

Petitioning (1 Kings 8:54)

Petition—to "make or present a formal request to (an authority) with respect to a particular cause"[3]

Interceding (1 Tim. 2:1–2)

Intercession—the action of saying a prayer on behalf of another person

The list of different types of prayer can actually be found in Scripture (1 Tim. 2:1), and it's safe to say it is there for a reason. We need to find out what each prayer means and offer up prayers to heaven that are in line with both God's Word and the courtroom. Heaven can't answer what is not according to God's will. The following verse can help you upgrade your understanding.

> I exhort therefore, that, first of all, supplications, prayers, intercessions, and giving of thanks, be made for all men.
>
> —1 TIMOTHY 2:1, KJV

MODEL PRAYERS OF THE PATRIARCHS

At this point I hope you're convinced of the reality of generational curses and the need to get free from them. But how do we pray effectively, and where do we begin? Well, three men in Scripture show us how to pray effectively to remove deep curses: their names are Ezra, Nehemiah, and

Daniel! Even though these men were known for other great achievements in the kingdom, those great breakthroughs would not have been accomplished without the intercessory prayers they prayed. I'm going to highlight them here without being exhaustive. Let's see how they prayed.

1. Prayer of Ezra: Recognize

During the time of Ezra we find him praying a prayer of repentance to God for the sins of the returned exiles who intermarried with the women from the surrounding nations. Ezra was so disappointed at the priest that he tore his clothes and pulled his beard.

> When I heard this, I tore my cloak and my shirt, pulled hair from my head and beard, and sat down utterly shocked. Then all who trembled at the words of the God of Israel came and sat with me because of this outrage committed by the returned exiles. And I sat there utterly appalled until the time of the evening sacrifice.
>
> —EZRA 9:3–4

This dramatic display of behavior by Ezra was considered an expression of recognition in ancient times for some inner conflict. It wasn't uncommon to see worshippers of YHWH tear their clothes in repentance when they became aware of their sin.

Being delivered from generational curses starts with *recognizing* the need to be free of deep sins and curses. Ezra, immediately after recognizing the sins of the priesthood, began confessing them and asking God to forgive them for their ignorance, in spite of going back into sin after coming out of seventy years of captivity.

> From the days of our ancestors until now, we have been *steeped in sin*. That is why we and our kings and our priests have been at the mercy of the pagan kings of the land. We have been killed, captured, robbed, and disgraced, just as we are today.
>
> —Ezra 9:7

You must go beyond just confession of normal sin and go right to the root. Ezra went deeper than the average prayers of repentance and began confessing the sin of his ancestors. There is no need for you to go that deep when looking to be free, but going a little ways back to find out what could be at the root of your family curses is necessary.

PRAYER OF FREEDOM

> *O God, I have sinned before You, in Your sight. My family and I have sinned. I'm asking You to forgive my sin of _____ (name the sin the Holy Spirit reveals to you). Lord Jesus, please set me free from the curse in my bloodline. I humbly ask that You would go deeper and reveal any other sin I'm unaware of, in Jesus' name!*

2. Prayer of Nehemiah: Write it down

Next we see Nehemiah also dealing with the exiles who returned to help build the wall, and yet again the work was held up because the people and the priest had sinned by intermarrying with foreigners. Nehemiah held a solemn assembly with everyone and began a time of confession that lasted six hours. I love this because true freedom isn't always instant. I know that many ministers—especially those who don't do deliverance—will say that it's instant. But those of us who really conduct deliverance know that at times, to help someone truly get free from a generational curse, it might take hours—hours of seeking God to reveal what is at the root.

> They remained standing in place for three hours while the Book of the Law of the LORD their God was read aloud to them. Then for three more hours they confessed their sins and worshiped the LORD their God.
>
> —NEHEMIAH 9:3

The deliverance session that Nehemiah led the people through lasted for six hours. Sometimes it will take that long to get to the root of a problem, but no matter how long it takes, stick it out! Don't give up! God is going to give the answer and bring breakthrough.

The question that should be asked is, "What did they do for all those six hours of confession?" The following verse tells you: they were writing! There were writing their sins and writing their repentance and promises. The next step to take while you're seeking deeper cleansing from curses is to have a pad and pen and write down what God shows you. *Put it in writing!* Write and write and write and write—and keep writing until you reach the core. Then begin to renounce and repent for all the curses written.

> The people responded, "In view of all this, we are making a solemn promise and putting it in *writing*. On this sealed document are the names of our leaders and Levites and priests."
>
> —NEHEMIAH 9:38

PRAYER OF FREEDOM

Holy Spirit, I'm going to spend the next couple of hours seeking Your face in prayer. I ask that as I seek You, You will begin to reveal what I need to repent of and renounce. I'm here with my pad and pen, ready for You to speak, in Jesus' name!

Note: Bookmark this page so you can pick up where you left off reading when you come back from your time with God!

3. Prayer of Daniel: Remind

The prophet Daniel also found himself in the same place Ezra and Nehemiah were in. Also, I don't find it a coincidence that all three of their prayers are in chapter 9 of the books that bear their names. Daniel begins to make confession to the Lord for all the people's sins, but instead of leaving it as just a prayer of confession and repentance, he takes it a step further and *reminds* God of His faithfulness. He reminds God about the covenant He made with Israel.

He reminds God of just how merciful He truly is with His people because He loves them.

What does this mean for us seeking freedom? We remind God of what He did for us by sending His Son, Jesus Christ, to die for our sins. Jesus is God's mercy toward us! At the center of all deliverance is Jesus! Remind heaven that mercy is extended to us through what Christ did on the cross.

> "O my God, lean down and listen to me. Open your eyes and see our despair. See how your city—the city that bears your name—lies in ruins. We make this plea, not because we deserve help, but because of your mercy. O Lord, hear. O Lord, forgive. O Lord, listen and act! For your own sake, do not delay, O my God, for your people and your city bear your name."...After this period of sixty-two sets of seven, the Anointed One will be killed, appearing to have accomplished nothing, and a ruler will arise whose armies will destroy the city and the Temple. The end will come with a flood, and war and its miseries are decreed from that time to the very end.
>
> —DANIEL 9:18–19, 26

As you can see, Daniel's prayer was sprinkled with reminders of just how merciful God is. When you spend time seeking God, take time to remind Him (through His Word) of the promises He made toward us, His people, and you will find a swifter outcome. Read what happened after

Daniel's prayer; the Bible says that Gabriel came swiftly to answer.

> As I was praying, Gabriel, whom I had seen in the earlier vision, came swiftly to me at the time of the evening sacrifice. He explained to me, "Daniel, I have come here to give you insight and understanding. The moment you began praying, a command was given. And now I am here to tell you what it was, for you are very precious to God. Listen carefully so that you can understand the meaning of your vision."
>
> —DANIEL 9:21–23

PRAYER OF FREEDOM

Normally I guide you in what to pray, but this time I'm going to allow you to pray in your own words of confession and remind God of His faithfulness.

ABRAHAM: THE MAN WHO NEGOTIATED WITH GOD

There is one story in Scripture that gives a bit more insight into how to move legally in prayer when we need an answer from God our Judge concerning the potential generational curses we need resolved. It is found in the story of Abraham and the visitors who came to see him while on their way to Sodom and Gomorrah.

READ GENESIS 18—THE WHOLE CHAPTER

While others see this story as nothing more than a historical moment between God and Abraham, it is actually one of the greatest courtroom deliberations found in Scripture, where man is pleading with the Judge to change his mind and is able to get God to change His mind at least three times.

We find King David doing the same thing when he sins with Bathsheba and their child is sick. David appeals to the courtroom of heaven to get God to change His mind. (But in this instance, God didn't change His mind and allowed the child to die.) King Hezekiah also deliberates with the courtroom of heaven and tells the Judge to remember His good deed and grant him more years of life. (His request was granted, and his life was extended fifteen more years.)

In the following verse we first see Abraham deliberating with God and two angels concerning His purpose for Sodom and Gomorrah. I love this text because it shows a mere human negotiating with God, and God agreeing to Abraham's terms. Though this event in Genesis 18 was a real-life occurrence in the life of Abraham, I think it was also placed in Scripture for us to read as a prescriptive example to follow. Now that you've read Genesis 18, you will notice five things: *posture, persistence, patience, pronouncement,* and *petition.* Let's go into the details by looking at each of these.

Posture—"a particular way of dealing with or considering something; an approach or attitude"[4]

If you look closely, you'll notice that the first thing Abraham does when he realizes who these three men are is hurry to approach them and bow low to the ground. This posture set him up to have an audience with God. Many times believers' hearts are in the right place, but their posture is off. Their lack of proper posture can grieve the heart of God and ruin a moment. As you seek the Lord to reveal where potential generational curses might be active in your life, your posture before the courtroom of heaven must be that of sincere humility and eagerness to obey when God reveals the root cause of the curse.

Abraham bowed low and gained an audience with God in one of the few times in Scripture where the Judge came down as the preincarnate Christ (also called the Angel of the Lord). Are you willing to humble yourself and seek the Lord for as long as it takes? Generational curses are not easily revealed; they require time and moments of seeking heaven to reveal. Right now, as you read this book, switch your posture. It doesn't matter where you are; you can posture your heart before the Lord, and He will meet you. God is passing through as you read this book—don't miss it. Abram knew what he had to do and did it, and the greatest story of a human deliberating with God over the affairs of mankind was the result.

> He looked up and noticed three men standing nearby. When he saw them, he ran to meet them and welcomed them, bowing low to the ground.

"My lord," he said, "if it pleases you, stop here for a while. Rest in the shade of this tree while water is brought to wash your feet."

—GENESIS 18:2–3

PRAYER FOR POSTURE

Heavenly Father, I know that right now You're with me as I read this book. May my posture be pleasing to You and cause You to draw near and hear my petition. Holy Spirit, help me to always keep a posture that is pleasing before You. In Jesus' name, amen.

Persistence—"firm or obstinate continuance in a course of action in spite of difficulty"[5]

Abraham's next act is persistence. Whereas most believers give up after one or two tries, Abraham didn't give up. He was persistent. If you read the story, you discover that the Lord and the two angels weren't there to visit Abraham; they were there to visit Sodom and see if the city was deemed worthy of being condemned—*but* Abraham persisted in persuading the Lord to stay for dinner. If you're going to get your generational curses dealt with, you have to be persistent in prayer, persistent in seeking, and persistent in asking God to reveal what is the root cause of your issue.

Most believers haven't been trained to be this persistent, but this book is designed to help you break out of that lazy form of Christianity and really seek the Lord. You've been sitting under that curse for too long, and it's time to get it revoked. Abraham was persistent! Never quit in seeking God for an answer. This story moves me because it shows that heaven doesn't mind dialoguing with us if we will just persist in His presence. Look at the following verses and see how Abraham persisted.

> ...Bowing low to the ground. "My lord," he said, "if it pleases you, stop here for a while. Rest in the shade of this tree while water is brought to wash your feet."
>
> —GENESIS 18:2–4

> When the food was ready, Abraham took some yogurt and milk and the roasted meat, and he served it to the men.
>
> —GENESIS 18:8

PRAYER FOR PERSISTENCE

Holy Spirit, help me to become persistent in prayer so that I would seek You until I get an answer. Strengthen me to be strong in my resolution to find the root cause of this generational curse. Lord Jesus, You're the curse breaker and my Advocate. Help me to be persistent, in Jesus' name.

Patience—"the capacity to accept or tolerate delay, trouble, or suffering without getting angry"[6]

Patience is a fruit of the Spirit and will be what's needed while your case goes to trial, figuratively speaking. All cases take time to go to trial. Some generational curses are easily revealed (the Holy Spirit at times will reveal them a lot sooner than expected), but for others it's not so easy. Delay in Scripture produces one fruit: patience! Abraham waited for his guests to finish eating, and many of you will have to wait in prayer or just move on with your normal day-to-day activities until heaven is ready to speak. I'm sure Abraham must have been anxious. The waiting process is always difficult, but Scripture tells us to be anxious for nothing and instead "let your requests [prayers] be made known to God; and the peace of God, which surpasses all understanding, will guard your hearts and minds through Christ Jesus" (Phil. 4:6–7, NKJV).

> As they ate, Abraham waited on them in the shade of the trees.
>
> —GENESIS 18:8

In the parable of the unjust judge, Jesus states the reason why God doesn't always answer so quickly:

> The judge ignored her for a while, but finally he said to himself...."I'm going to see that she gets justice, because she is wearing me out with her constant requests!"
>
> ...Learn a lesson from this unjust judge. Even he rendered a just decision in the end. So don't you think God will surely give justice to his chosen people who cry out to him day and night? Will he keep putting them off? I tell you, he will grant justice to them quickly! But when the Son

of Man returns, how many will he find on the
earth who have faith?

—Luke 18:4–8

During this season while you wait for the Holy Spirit to
speak, allow the fruit of patience to be developed as James 1:4
says: "But let patience have her perfect work [in you]" (KJV).

Pronouncement—"a formal or authoritative announcement or declaration"[7]

In court, a pronouncement is a legally binding decision
and will be recorded by the court clerk, who also makes
note of when it occurred and who was present at the time.
Here is where this story with Abraham takes a different
turn: the Lord finally speaks and says, "Shall I hide from
Abraham what I am about to do?" (Gen. 18:17, ESV). I'm
here to tell you, your answer is on its way. Just when you
least expect it, the Lord will visit and share with you the
pronouncement of what's been holding you and your family back and how to resolve it.

> Then the men got up from their meal and looked
> out toward Sodom. As they left, Abraham went
> with them to send them on their way. "Should I
> hide my plan from Abraham?" the Lord asked....
> So the Lord told Abraham, "I have heard a great
> outcry from Sodom and Gomorrah, because their
> sin is so flagrant. I am going down to see if their
> actions are as wicked as I have heard. If not, I want
> to know."

—Genesis 18:16–17, 20–21

These verses bring me great joy in knowing there is an answer from heaven. We won't spend the rest of our days trying to figure out what's wrong or what the root is. The Lord, through the Holy Spirit, will find a way to give us an answer.

Petition—to "make or present a formal request to (an authority) with respect to a particular cause"[8]

And finally, once Abraham knew that God had spoken to him on what was the real reason for the visit to his region, he proceeded to deliberate with God concerning the case against Sodom. In the court it's called petition. A petition is "*a formal request seeking a court order and stating the reasons why it is needed.*"[9] It may be filed by a person, a group, or an organization, and is typically the first step in a lawsuit. A petition also may be used to appeal a court's decision. Look at these verses and see how many times Abraham petitioned the Lord to sway His decision, and in each instance the Lord did change His mind.

> Abraham approached him and said, "Will you sweep away both the righteous and the wicked? Suppose you find fifty righteous people living there in the city—will you still sweep it away and not spare it for their sakes? Surely you wouldn't do such a thing, destroying the righteous along with the wicked. Why, you would be treating the righteous and the wicked exactly the same! Surely you wouldn't do that! Should not the Judge of all the earth do what is right?" And the LORD replied, "If I find fifty righteous people in

Sodom, I will spare the entire city for their sake." Then Abraham spoke again. "Since I have begun, let me speak further to my Lord, even though I am but dust and ashes. Suppose there are only forty-five righteous people rather than fifty? Will you destroy the whole city for lack of five?" And the LORD said, "I will not destroy it if I find forty-five righteous people there." Then Abraham pressed his request further. "Suppose there are only forty?" And the LORD replied, "I will not destroy it for the sake of the forty."

"Please don't be angry, my Lord," Abraham pleaded. "Let me speak—suppose only thirty righteous people are found?" And the LORD replied, "I will not destroy it if I find thirty." Then Abraham said, "Since I have dared to speak to the Lord, let me continue—suppose there are only twenty?" And the LORD replied, "Then I will not destroy it for the sake of the twenty." Finally, Abraham said, "Lord, please don't be angry with me if I speak one more time. Suppose only ten are found there?" And the LORD replied, "Then I will not destroy it for the sake of the ten."

—GENESIS 18:23–32

What I love about our beautiful Savior is that He can be persuaded to change His mind because of His love for us! Once the curse has been revealed to you, you then have the legal right to petition the court to reverse its decision. Once the Holy Spirit tells you what the generational curse is, you can roll up your sleeves and bombard the courtroom to change its mind. Having revelation of what curse is operating in your life gives you an advantage because you can be strategic, and your prayers will be more effective and see results. Has the Lord shown you what curse might be operating in your life? If so, now it's time to go to war with what God showed you.

GENERATIONAL BLESSINGS

I know this book has been heavy in revealing generational curses, and it may seem like the theme is centered only on the negative, but remember that God pours out generational blessings on His people—even someone like me. Many of you reading this know my story, but for those who don't, here's a recap: I'm an ex-convict who got saved while serving a nine-year prison sentence. (My conversion story has been featured on *The 700 Club*.) I had a radical encounter with Christ and began to live for Him behind bars. When I was released from prison in 1998, I continued to serve the Lord. Now all these years later I'm still serving the Lord.

I've watched heaven break the generational curses in my life, and I've been the recipient of His blessing. He broke the curse of poverty on my life. Today I'm a best-selling author, and I've traveled the world teaching this message of deliverance. I've been on every major Christian television network sharing deliverance, I've sat with kings in African nations and prayed God's blessing over them, and I've ministered deliverance to celebrities and influential people. I'm married to a beautiful woman, Ibelize Pagani, and we have two children, Apollos and Xavier. God does indeed give generational blessings! I've watched my family get blessed because of my service to God.

> On that day a fountain will be opened for the
> dynasty [bloodline] of David and for the people
> of Jerusalem, a fountain to cleanse them from all
> their sins and impurity.
>
> —ZECHARIAH 13:1

Make the choice to live for God, and watch Him pour out blessings that will be extended to a thousand generations. Say like Joshua, "As for me and my house, we will serve the LORD" (Josh. 24:15, ESV).

CONCLUDING THOUGHTS

As we close this chapter, allow the model prayers of these Old Testament patriarchs that we covered to encourage you to deepen your times of prayer. These secrets have been given for a reason, and they are for us to follow. We don't have to pray original prayers when we spend time seeking God; we can also use Scripture and the very same prayers these men prayed and get immediate results. God is challenging you to move beyond just praying the psalms, even though there's nothing wrong with that. Scripture holds a vast ocean of prayers we can draw from to remove deep curses. Ask the Holy Spirit to point these out to you, and make it your business to model them!

CHAPTER 10

STRATEGIES TO KEEP THE BLOODLINE CLEANSED

Today I have given you the choice between life and death, between blessings and *curses*. Now I call on heaven and earth to witness the choice you make. Oh, that you would choose life, so that you and your descendants might live! You can make this choice by loving the LORD your God, obeying him, and committing yourself firmly to him.

—DEUTERONOMY 30:19–20

Because we have these promises, dear friends, let us cleanse ourselves from everything that can defile our body or spirit. And let us work toward complete holiness because we fear God.

—2 CORINTHIANS 7:1

NOW THAT WE are at the end of the book, the opening verses in Deuteronomy are clear and reveal God's overall intention for you and your bloodline. *God wants you to choose life and blessing!* And He desires to bless you! But that blessing is conditional, and it's found in one phrase of the first verse we just read: "Oh, that you would choose life." This implies that God is hoping you will make the right decision in choosing life but also by making sure the door to generational curses stays closed for future generations.

In this chapter we will go over some strategies to help you keep the door closed permanently.

The apostle Paul encouraged the Corinthian believers to cleanse themselves from everything that can defile the body and spirit, "perfecting holiness in the fear of God" (2 Cor. 7:1, KJV). That means this "cleansing" can only come through an initial effort on our part in pursuing holiness. *Holiness must be intentional!* We don't stumble our way to holiness; rather, with the help of the Holy Spirit we *work* our way to holiness. The Bible says to "work out" our own salvation with fear and trembling (Phil. 2:12). This chapter is going to give you some strategies to implement to keep your bloodline cleansed.

Scripture records the stories of people whose lives are an example for us to follow in moments of intense crisis. In the history of Israel, the story of one particular father and his grandson makes a bold underline to everything we've been learning about the courtroom of heaven and the possibility of reformation. I'm referring to King Manasseh and his grandson King Josiah. In my opinion, this family brought the greatest reformation the children of Israel had ever seen during a season when they were steeped in idolatry. I believe their militant actions reflect how believers should be toward keeping their bloodlines cleansed through the power of Jesus' name. I know these two personalities aren't as popular as Elijah, Moses, Joshua, or David, but they are the most important when it comes to reformation.

MANASSEH'S REFORMATION THROUGH PLEA: STRATEGY #1

Manasseh is considered by many to be the most wicked king who ever reigned in Israel. His reign lasted fifty-two years, and for most of that time the Bible says he was wicked before the eyes of the Lord and caused Israel to sin. He practiced worship of Molech, which was an abomination, and set up idols all over Israel, even in the temple of YHWH. He had shrines with temple prostitutes all over the land. And during his reign Israel was heavily oppressed. He did not follow after the ways of his father, King Hezekiah. Up to this point the nation had never been subject to so many years of idolatry under one king. Manasseh was the longest-reigning idolatrous king in the history of Israel.

Toward the end of Manasseh's reign, God had enough and sent him into captivity to the Assyrian army, which was known to be cruel to those they conquered. Scripture doesn't record this, but we can speculate that they oppressed King Manasseh to the point that he repented for all of his idolatries and *pleaded* with God for mercy.

What's interesting about this text is that Manasseh's prayer wasn't just any prayer; Scripture says it was an "entreaty" (2 Chron. 33:13, NIV). The meaning of this word is found in the legal term *plea*, which means a deal. I personally know what this means, as back in 1993 I was facing seven to twenty-one years for a string of armed robberies, and after eighteen months of taking my cases to trial, the judge offered me a *plea bargain*—meaning he would give me a lighter sentence on the terms that I would plead guilty.

I readily took that "deal," and instead of spending up to twenty-one years in prison, I was sentenced to only nine years. Bronx County and I made a deal through a plea, an entreaty!

King Manasseh made a deal with the God of Israel. Our sacred canon doesn't record this prayer, but it states that it was documented in the annals of the kings of Israel (2 Chron. 33:18). Such prayers were only documented if they were of great significance. I'm sure this prayer included a deal between Manasseh and God, and I think it's safe to say it was more along the lines of "God, if You deliver me from the slavery of the Assyrians, I will undo and remove everything I did that caused this." Look at the following verses.

> So the LORD brought against them the army commanders of the king of Assyria, who took Manasseh prisoner, put a hook in his nose, bound him with bronze shackles and took him to Babylon. In his distress he sought the favor of the LORD his God and humbled himself greatly before the God of his ancestors. And when he prayed to him, the LORD was moved by his *entreaty* and listened to his *plea*; so he brought him back to Jerusalem and to his kingdom. Then Manasseh knew that the LORD is God.
>
> —2 CHRONICLES 33:11–13, NIV

King Manasseh's plea in the courtroom of heaven moved God so much that the Lord swiftly delivered him, and he was sent back to Israel, where he fulfilled his part of the plea bargain and dismantled the idolatry he had initiated.

Manasseh's public repentance must have been an inspiration to witness, as the once idolatrous king was now destroying the very idols he'd formerly served. This reformation might not have changed all of Israel, nor removed all the idols that were deeply entrenched in Israel, but his public repentance was a great start and the impetus for God's revealing the strategy to get the nation to return to its former glory.

So the first step in bringing reformation and keeping your bloodline cleansed is pleading with God through *drastic repentance*. It needs to be done in accordance with the model of the Lord's Prayer. Jesus said when you pray, you are to say, "Forgive us our sins, as we forgive those who sin against us" (Luke 11:4). This part of the Lord's Prayer is centered around going before His throne of grace and allowing the Holy Spirit to reveal where you and your family keep missing it.

Repentance is more than just saying, "I'm sorry." The biblical definition of repentance is a one-eighty turnaround, to completely change your mind. John the Baptist went further when he was addressing the Pharisees who repented by saying "show fruits" worthy of repentance. (See Luke 3:7–9.) Fruit takes time to grow. While I believe repentance can be instant, I also believe that sometimes a believer might need to go through a season of repentance and supplication before the Lord.

King Manasseh was truly repentant and prayed hard for the Lord to forgive him for causing Israel to sin. I'm sure his prayer wasn't an instant prayer but rather a prayer filled with godly sorrow and reflection for what he had done, and he waited for God to show him what needed to be done to undo the works of darkness on his bloodline. Unfortunately, while God had mercy on Manasseh personally, the idolatry he perpetrated was so entrenched that it created a generational curse, and the nation of Israel would be judged by seventy years of exile in the future.

Right now, get a piece of paper and pen and ask the Lord Jesus to reveal the areas you need to repent of and where there is stubborn and deeply entrenched sin for which you need to repent. For many of you this will require making a public confession to your family through family devotions or family intervention. Others who are serving in ministry may need to repent publicly to your church for years of secret sinful behavior. (Some of you may need to step down and away from ministry for a season or indefinitely.)

The prayer of Manasseh was not done half-heartedly. This level of drastic repentance might need drastic actions to accompany it, as was the case with King Manasseh. For married couples who have been secretly unfaithful, you will need to muster up all the strength God gives you and openly admit to your spouse your adulterous affair, no matter what the consequences may be. I'm sure Manasseh counted the cost of publicly repenting of his idolatry, but it was worth it. This level of repentance will cause a swift change, as God will fulfill His end of your plea deal. As the Holy Spirit reveals what needs to be repented of, write it down, and go through each item and verbally renounce it. As you do, the Holy Spirit will give you a strategy and show you how to close the door. Allow this prayer to be a guide, but pray it in your own words.

PRAYER OF ENTREATY

> *Lord God, Judge of all creation, I come before Your throne of grace to ask for forgiveness for all the iniquity I have committed throughout the years that has caused others to be affected. I wholeheartedly turn from those things. I plead before Your heavenly court in the name of Jesus that You would revoke all that was done and restore all who were affected. As King Manasseh drastically repented, I also repent and make a covenant with You today that I will never do those things again and will make restitution to everyone You require of me! Holy Spirit, please answer me as You did Manasseh, and seal this pleading with the precious blood of Jesus! (Keep praying in your own words as the Holy Spirit guides you.)*

JOSIAH'S REFORMATION: STRATEGY #2

One of the greatest of all the kings of Judah was Josiah. His birth was prophesied three hundred years before by a young prophet who declared that during his reign Josiah would bring the greatest religious reform to the temple and Judah the nation had ever seen. (This is a type of deliverance and dismantling of generational curses.)

At the LORD's command, a man of God from Judah went to Bethel, arriving there just as Jeroboam was approaching the altar to burn incense. Then at the LORD's command, he shouted, "O altar, altar! This is what the LORD says: A child named Josiah will be born into the dynasty of David. On you he will sacrifice the priests from the pagan shrines who come here to burn incense, and human bones will be burned on you." That same day the man of God gave a sign to prove his message. He said, "The LORD has promised to give this sign: This altar will split apart, and its ashes will be poured out on the ground."

—1 KINGS 13:1–3

This prophecy would be fulfilled three hundred years later as the Babylonian exile was approaching. Though the territory of Judah had the greatest number of kings that pleased the Lord, it also had some of the worst kings that ever existed for both the northern and southern kingdoms, as the children of Israel would mess up again and again and return to idolatry after periods of repentance and reformation.

These disasters happened to Judah because of the LORD's command. He had decided to banish Judah from his presence because of the *many sins* of Manasseh, who had filled Jerusalem with innocent blood. The LORD would not forgive this.

—2 KINGS 24:3–4

Many years later this curse was fulfilled, just as the Lord had promised to those who refused to obey Him—and we see the third and fourth generations of King Manasseh's dynasty suffering the consequences. During the time of the prophets Zephaniah and Jeremiah a descendant was born (grandson of King Manasseh) named Josiah. Very early in Josiah's reign God put it on his heart to thoroughly cleanse the land of seven hundred years of idolatry King Jeroboam had initiated in the northern kingdom, which had also gained a foothold in the southern kingdom. As a fulfillment of prophecy, the mantle for reformation came upon Josiah, and no other king cleansed the land with so much zeal.

Using the typology mentioned earlier in this book, through Josiah we see a thorough cleansing of not only stopping the acts of idolatry but also dismantling the systems of support. True reform requires undoing the system by which the acts are given legal right to function. Without a system in place and a designated location where that system was stationed, the priest and temple prostitutes could not function, nor could worship through sacrificial offerings to Baal, Asherah, and the powers of the heavens be carried out.

Josiah was an important figure, as he represented the removing of the systems that granted Satan legal access to gain a foothold in Judah. And just as his grandfather King Manasseh had begun a reformation, he would continue his efforts but would go harder—harder than any other king before him. King Josiah's reform was so intense that he even burned the bones of the pagan priests.

> During the eighth year of his reign, while he was still young, Josiah began to seek the God of his ancestor David. Then in the twelfth year he began to purify Judah and Jerusalem, destroying all the pagan shrines, the Asherah poles, and the carved idols and cast images. He ordered that the altars of Baal be demolished and that the incense altars which stood above them be broken down. He also made sure that the Asherah poles, the carved idols, and the cast images were smashed and scattered over the graves of those who had sacrificed to them. He burned the bones of the pagan priests on their own altars, and so he purified Judah and Jerusalem.
>
> —2 CHRONICLES 34:3–5

This Scripture passage depicts the second step necessary to bringing reformation to your life and keeping your bloodline cleansed, and it's called *drastic removal*. Right now get a piece of paper and a pen, open your Bible, and ask the Holy Spirit to reveal to you all areas where an open door could be causing sin, and write them down. And just as King Josiah waged a campaign to tear down those idolatrous altars that his grandfather was not able to remove, wholeheartedly repent for those generational sins as the Word of God brings conviction of the Holy Spirit. Afterward, renounce any legal doors given to the enemy either through ignorance or willful transgression and verbally command that any demons and strongmen must leave your life in the name of Jesus. (Take your time doing this.)

Next, go through your home, or gather your family for prayer and intervention, and share with them what the Holy Spirit has revealed about the family's sins. Together make intercession to the courtroom of heaven (you lead the prayer, unless there is a stronger believer in your immediate family), and as a family make an *entreaty* before your heavenly Father. If you need to have a small season of fasting and prayer as a family, do it! There have been seasons where as a family we've fasted for longer than fifty days, and we've seen God move on our family's behalf as we've made bargains with God (plea deals) on particular behaviors we would follow if heaven would answer on our behalf.

Now, I'm not saying you must fast and pray in such drastic ways as my family and I have done. But what I am saying is that sometimes you might need to—or rather the Holy Spirit might require you to. Why? Because Jesus said "this kind does not go out except by prayer and fasting" (Mark 17:21, NKJV). Allow the following prayer to serve as a guide

PRAYER OF REFORMATION

Heavenly Father, grant me the strength to bring drastic change to all works of darkness that You reveal need to be undone. Holy Spirit, I ask that You grant me the strength, like Josiah, to bring great reformation and the change needed to put everything in order according to Your original design. Grant me the boldness to make the necessary changes with no fear, in Jesus' name! (Keep

praying in your own words as the Holy Spirit
guides you.)

ASK CHRIST TO INTERCEDE: STRATEGY #3

Many years ago I was going through a really rough time
in ministry. We had been pioneering a path for deliverance,
and it had been extremely difficult, as churches, leaders, and
movements were hostile to it. I grew increasingly discouraged and even considered giving up and focusing on other
areas of ministry. No matter how much I prayed, no matter how much I fasted, and no matter how much I quoted
Scripture, I couldn't break through. This carried on for a
long season where it felt like the heavens were brass and I
couldn't sense any breakthrough (even though I didn't need
any personal deliverance and had no open doors).

One day while I was praying on the altar at church and
telling God just how defeated I felt, the Holy Spirit inspired
a thought to ask Jesus to intercede for me. Immediately
the following verse came to my mind, and it dawned on
me that Jesus is not only the Savior of my sins but also my
High Priest; He can intercede for us and get results. At that
time it had never occurred to me to request prayer from
Jesus.

I prayed a simple prayer: "Lord Jesus, I'm so discouraged
right now, and I don't know what I'm doing wrong, but as
my High Priest, I ask that You pray to the Father on my
behalf because I don't even know what to pray for." Within
a couple of minutes of praying that simple prayer, an over-
whelming peace enveloped me, and it lingered tangibly

upon me for the rest of that season. Look at what the Book of Hebrews says:

> But because Jesus lives forever, he has a perma-
> nent priesthood. Therefore he is able to save com-
> pletely those who come to God through him,
> because he always lives to intercede for them.
> Such a high priest truly meets our need—one
> who is holy, blameless, pure, set apart from sin-
> ners, exalted above the heavens.
>
> —HEBREWS 7:24–26, NIV

We're not helpless believers who have been given a bunch of Christian rules and regulations and left to fend for ourselves trying to fulfill them. The text here says that we have a personal, direct connection to Jesus, who serves as our High Priest. I know that this type of prayer is not what we're used to, but it's biblical. In the Old Testament all high priests were ordained by God to stand as mediators between the people and God. They would offer sacrifices on behalf of the people who came looking for atonement for daily sins. The priest would stand before God and offer up their sacrifices, but he would also plead with God for them because he understood the necessity of being forgiven.

Christ, who is God manifested in the flesh, became a man and took on the feeling of our infirmities and was tempted in all points as we are. So Christ completely understands and is able to sympathize and empathize with our human struggle and different temptations. The great thing about pleading directly to our Great Intercessor is that "he ever liveth to make intercession for [us]" (v. 25, KJV), meaning that His role and function as our High Priest will remain eternal, and therefore He will always stand in the gap on our behalf. We can confidently trust Him to continue to plead for us, even when we have more strength to plead for ourselves. Jesus never gets tired, He never wavers, He never changes his mind. We can daily pray to Jesus and ask Him to plead to the heavenly court on our behalf, knowing that whatever He asks, His heavenly Father (who is our heavenly Father) grants it to Him. Pray the following prayer right now.

PRAYER OF INTERCESSION TO OUR HIGH PRIEST

Lord Jesus, thank You for being my High Priest. I'm humbly asking that You would intercede for me right now, and for my household. Strengthen us to fulfill Your will and to walk in true holiness. Empower us to walk in all that is outlined in Scripture and to stand against the wiles of the devil. (Keep praying in your own words as the Holy Spirit guides you.)

GET AWAY FROM THE TENTS OF KORAH: STRATEGY #4

The next way we can ensure longevity is by planting ourselves away from those who have the curse of the Lord upon them. I'm not referring to having a phobia of being around people, but I am saying that we need to pray more and be more cautious about who we partner with in relationships, business, church, covering, and so forth. To partner with such an individual is to place ourselves under the same curse they are under.

In Numbers 16 we find 250 influential men being led by Korah in coming against Moses.

> One day Korah son of Izhar, a descendant of Kohath son of Levi, conspired with Dathan and Abiram, the sons of Eliab, and On the son of Peleth, from the tribe of Reuben. They incited a rebellion against Moses, along with 250 other leaders of the community, all prominent members of the assembly. They united against Moses and Aaron and said, "You have gone too far! The whole community of Israel has been set apart by the LORD, and he is with all of us. What right do you have to act as though you are greater than the rest of the LORD's people?"
>
> —NUMBERS 16:1–3

The Lord was so displeased with Korah's actions that He judged these men and also their families and anyone else who joined in his rebellion against Moses. The Lord told Moses to tell the children of Israel, "Get away from the tents of Korah," implying that swift judgment was coming, not just to them but to their homes.

> And the LORD said to Moses, "Then tell all
> the people to get away from the tents of Korah,
> Dathan, and Abiram."
>
> —NUMBERS 16:23–24

It's one thing to tell everyone to remove themselves from the presence of the guilty party, but heaven sent judgment against their whole families. This meant anyone living in their homes or even coming by to visit that day would die. The end result of this story was that the curse of the Lord came upon everyone and everything they owned.

> He had hardly finished speaking the words when
> the ground suddenly split open beneath them.
> The earth opened its mouth and swallowed the
> men, along with their households and all their
> followers who were standing with them, and
> everything they owned.
>
> —NUMBERS 16:31–32

The admonition is clear: stay away from those whose lives aren't in full obedience to God's Word because there could be collateral damage. Pray about all relationships. Pray about all business partnerships. Allow the Holy Spirit to give you discernment about the ministries that you sit under or allow to nourish you spiritually. Many years ago, in my early days of pastoring, I sat under an apostolic covering for a season that proved to be manipulative, and during that time my life started going downhill. (Please know that I believe in modern apostles; most apostolic ministries aren't like that one.) My finances dried up. My wife and I were arguing all the time. Several leaders left our church or chose to stay home while we were serving under said covering. It wasn't until our marriage was at the point of divorce that it dawned on me that the beginning of our marriage, pastoral, and family issues could be traced to one defining moment—when we connected with that covering!

We held a family meeting and decided to leave this church, and when we did I immediately sensed a sigh of relief in the spirit. Soon after, the blessing of the Lord started coming back to our home, and our marriage hasn't suffered any fights leading to divorce since. I can't stress this fourth strategy enough. If this requires you to downsize some of your friendships, then do so (if and only if you discern such friends are toxic for your Christian experience). Just make sure you're not unequally yoked together with unbelievers. Now, I'm not saying you should be mean, hostile, or critical toward such persons, but what I am saying is that there is a huge difference between you and them. Look at the following verse:

> The LORD curses the house of the wicked, but he blesses the home of the upright.
>
> —PROVERBS 3:33

When you separate yourself from those who have the curse of the Lord over them, you're walking in *uprightness*, and you can be sure that God's favor and blessing will remain on you and your household for future generations.

PRAYER OF REPENTANCE

Heavenly Father, I repent for any and all forms of rebellion and usurpation that I may have been a part of both knowingly and unknowingly. I ask You to forgive me and my bloodline for walking in dishonor. I plead my household's case in the name of Jesus and ask that Jesus, my Advocate, would intercede on our behalf and resolve all violations against the courtroom of heaven. Holy Spirit, I want my house and family bloodline to be blessed, sanctified, and fulfilling God's purpose. Thank You, Jesus, for the work You did on the cross to sever all curses and the work You currently do as my Intercessor. I love You! In Jesus' name, amen. (Keep praying in your own words as the Holy Spirit guides you.)

GOD'S PROMISE TO NEVER ALLOW THE CURSE

As we close this book, we can end with God's promise found in the following verse:

> And Jerusalem will be filled, safe at last, never again to be cursed and destroyed.
>
> —ZECHARIAH 14:11

He will never allow the curse to touch us as we remain in Christ, living in obedience to the Scriptures and walking in true holiness, totally depending on the Holy Spirit. This is a great promise for us to stand on. We can rest knowing that God will be faithful to His promise. The curse will remain perpetually broken through Christ's work on the cross, and we can be assured that our household will be filled with the safety of God's presence as the Holy Spirit enforces that work of redemption and sanctification. Allow the promise of Zechariah 14:11 to sink deep into your heart, and walk out the abundant life that Jesus promised us in John 10:10: "The thief does not come except to steal, and to kill, and to destroy. I have come that they may have life, and that they may have it more abundantly" (NKJV).

THE BLESSING OF OBED-EDOM

God wants to bless your house, but there is a requirement for that to happen. One of the best stories in Scripture to illustrate this is the account of the house of Obed-edom. During the time of King David, on the day he became king, the Philistines heard about the coronation and mobilized an army to attack David. David was given instruction by God on how to conquer them, and upon returning from his victory he decided to bring the ark of the covenant temporarily into the house of Obed-edom. (Backstory: a man named Uzzah had died trying to stabilize the fallen oxen carrying the ark.) While the ark was in Obed-edom's house for three months, God blessed him so notably that David fetched the ark and brought it to the city of David.

> So David decided not to move the Ark of the
> LORD into the City of David. Instead, he took it
> to the house of Obed-edom of Gath. The Ark of

> the LORD remained there in Obed-edom's house
> for three months, and the LORD blessed Obed-
> edom and his entire household.
>
> —2 SAMUEL 6:10–11

You must be intentional about housing the ark—the presence of God—in your home! There is no way around it. Obed-edom was intentional in allowing the ark to stay in his home, knowing that death was always the portion of those who wouldn't walk right around the ark. I'm sure that when David offered to have the ark stay at Obed-edom's house, at first Obed was fearful. But that fear was quickly extinguished because Obed decided that death wouldn't happen in his home if he decided to walk uprightly. The same is true with you. You must make the choice to live right and walk according to God's ways, knowing that when you do, your home will be blessed. Make a covenant with God right now that you're going to live for Him in such a way that you want heaven to choose your home for the presence of God to dwell in!

FINAL THOUGHTS

As we close this book, I hope that everything taught, revealed, and explained in it has enhanced your understanding of this topic of generational curses, iniquity, and finding freedom. The hard part is past in that this book challenged the way you think, confronted some falsehood in your worldview, and refuted unbiblical ideologies regarding generational curses. While most people can't handle this level of reformation, you survived because you're serious about breaking the curse in the bloodline. The courtroom of heaven has registered your effort and will take this into account for future reference. Jesus Christ cares about the future of your bloodline and wants you to be free and stay free. Let the words of John 8:36 (NKJV) sink deep within your soul: "If the Son makes you free, you shall be free indeed."

ACTS THAT CAN INITIATE CURSES

THERE ARE MANY ways a curse can be initiated in a person's life. I am listing several here, but keep in mind that many of these curses are broken when we accept the Lord Jesus Christ as our Savior. Others must be broken through the processes outlined in this book.

Cursing/mistreating Jews
(Gen. 12:3, 27:29; Num. 24:9; Deut. 27:26)

Willingly deceiving others
(Gen. 27:12; Josh. 9:23; Jer. 48:10; Mal. 1:14)

Committing adultery
(Num. 5:27; Deut. 22:22–27; Job 24:15–18)

Disobeying the Lord's commandments
(Deut. 11:28; Isa. 24:3–6; Jer. 11:3; Dan. 9:11)

Participating in idolatry
(Exod. 20:5; Deut. 5:8–9, 29:19; Jer. 44:8)

Keeping or owning cursed objects
(Deut. 7:25; Josh. 6:18)

Refusing to come to the Lord's help
(Judg. 5:23)

Having a wicked house
(Prov. 3:33)

Turning a blind eye to the poor
(Prov. 28:27)

Stealing and swearing falsely by the Lord's name
(Zech. 5:4)

Ministers failing to give the glory to God
(Mal. 2:2; Rev. 1:6)

Robbing God of tithes and offerings
(Hag. 1:6–9; Mal. 3:9)

Hearkening unto one's spouse rather than God
(Gen. 3:17)

Lightly esteeming one's parents
(Deut. 27:16)

Making graven images
(Exod. 20:4; Deut. 5:8; 27:15)

Willfully cheating people out of their property
(Deut. 27:17)

Taking advantage of the blind
(Deut. 27:18)

Oppressing strangers, widows, and the fatherless
(Exod. 22:22–24; Deut. 27:19)

Lying with one's father's wife
(Lev. 18:8; Deut. 27:20)

Lying with one's sister
(Deut. 27:22)

Smiting one's neighbors secretly
(Deut. 27:24)

Taking money to slay the innocent
(Deut. 27:24)

Lying with any beast
(Exod. 22:19; Deut. 27:21)

Being proud
(Ps. 119:21)

Trusting in man and not the Lord
(Jer. 48:10)

Doing the work of the Lord deceitfully
(Jer. 48:10)

Rewarding evil for good
(Prov. 17:13)

Being born out of wedlock
(Deut. 23:2)

Being born from incestuous unions
(Gen. 19:36–38)

Committing murder
(Exod. 21:12)

Committing indirect murder
(Exod. 21:14)

Striking one's parents
(Exod. 21:15)

Kidnapping someone
(Exod. 21:16; Deut. 24:7)

Cursing one's parents
(Exod. 21:17)

Causing the unborn to die
(Exod. 21:22–23)

Not preventing death
(Exod. 21:29)

Engaging in witchcraft
(Exod. 22:18)

Making sacrifices to false gods
(Exod. 22:20)

Attempting to turn people away from the Lord
(Deut. 13:6–9)

Following horoscopes
(Deut. 17:2–5)

Rebelling against God-ordained pastors
(Deut. 17:12)

Prophesying falsely
(Deut. 18:19–22)

Not keeping one's virginity until marriage
(Deut. 22:13–21)

Not disciplining one's children but honoring
them above God (1 Sam. 2:17, 27–36)

Cursing one's rulers
(Exod. 22:28; 1 Kings 2:8–9)

Teaching people to rebel against the Lord
(Jer. 28:16–17)

Refusing to warn those who sin
(Ezek. 3:18–21)

Defiling the Sabbath
(Exod. 31:14; Num. 15:32–36)

Sacrificing human beings
(Lev. 20:2)

Participating in séances and fortune-telling
(Lev. 20:6)

Engaging in homosexual and lesbian relationships
(Gen. 19:13, 24–25; Lev. 18:22, 20:13; Jude 7)

Blaspheming the Lord's name
(Lev. 24:15–16)

Being carnally minded
(Rom. 8:6)

Rebelling against one's parents
(Deut. 21:18–21)

Committing any sin worthy of death
(Deut. 21:22–23).

OTHER ACTIONS AND CIRCUMSTANCES THAT CAN BRING CURSES

This list is not exhaustive, but here are some common actions that may initiate curses in your life.

- Church splits
- Cursing
- Denial
- Dishonor / Dishonor to parents
- Dysfunction
- Hoarding
- Homosexuality
- Illegitimacy
- Intimidation
- Isolation
- Man-pleasing
- Masturbation
- Mocking
- Murmuring
- Narcissism
- Racism
- Ruin
- Slothfulness
- Wastefulness

NOTES

CHAPTER 1

1. Affixes, s.v. *"all(o),"* accessed May 3, 2023, https://www.affixes.org/alpha/a/allo-.html.
2. Affixes, s.v. *"all(o)."*
3. Blue Letter Bible, s.v. *"skia,"* accessed May 3, 2023, https://www.blueletterbible.org/lexicon/g4639/kjv/tr/0-1/.
4. Blue Letter Bible, s.v. *"typos,"* accessed May 3, 2023, https://www.blueletterbible.org/lexicon/g5179/kjv/tr/0-1/.
5. Bible Study Tools, s.v. *"ginomai,"* accessed May 3, 2023, https://www.biblestudytools.com/lexicons/greek/nas/ginomai.html.
6. "What Is Epigenetics?," Centers for Disease Control and Prevention, August 15, 2022, https://www.cdc.gov/genomics/disease/epigenetics.htm.

CHAPTER 2

1. King James Bible Dictionary, s.v. "Tubal," accessed May 3, 2023, https://kingjamesbibledictionary.com/Dictionary/Tubal.

2. Hitchcock's Bible Names Dictionary, s.v. "Cain," accessed May 3, 2023, https://www.ccel.org/ccel/hitchcock/bible_names.html?term=Cain.

3. Wikipedia, s.v. "Canaan (son of Ham)," accessed May 3, 2023, https://en.wikipedia.org/wiki/Canaan_(son_of_Ham).

4. King James Bible Dictionary, s.v. "Amorite," accessed May 3, 2023, https://kingjamesbibledictionary.com/Dictionary/Amorite.

5. Abarim Publications, s.v. "Hittite," accessed May 3, 2023, https://www.abarim-publications.com/Meaning/Hittite.html.

CHAPTER 3

1. Dr. Myles Munroe, *Kingdom Principles: Preparing for Kingdom Experience and Expansion* (Shippensburg, PA: Destiny Image, 2006).

2. Dictionary.com, s.v. "decree," accessed May 3, 2023, https://www.dictionary.com/browse/decree.

3. Ralph Levy, "What Is the Torah?," Life Hope & Truth, accessed May 3, 2023, https://lifehopeandtruth.com/bible/biblical-laws/what-is-the-torah/.

4. *Merriam-Webster*, s.v. "statute," accessed May 3, 2023, https://www.merriam-webster.com/dictionary/statute.

5. Online Etymology Dictionary, s.v. "statute," accessed May 3, 2023, https://www.etymonline.com/word/statute.

6. *Macmillan Dictionary*, s.v. "regulation," accessed May 3, 2023, https://www.macmillandictionary.com/us/dictionary/american/regulation_1.

7. Hebrew4Christians, s.v. *"mitzvah,"* accessed May 3, 2023, https://www.hebrew4christians.com/Glossary/Word_of_the_Week/Archived/Mitzvah/mitzvah.html.

8. The Free (Legal) Dictionary, s.v. "judgment," accessed May 3, 2023, https://legal-dictionary.thefreedictionary.com/judgment.

9. Hebrew Word Study–Skip Moen, s.v. *"eduth,"* January 15, 2011, https://skipmoen.com/tag/eduth/.

10. Vocabulary.com, s.v. "precept," accessed May 3, 2023, https://www.vocabulary.com/dictionary/precept.

11. "Concession Definition," yourdictionary.com, accessed May 3, 2023, https://www.yourdictionary.com/concession.

12. Rich Oka, "The Hebrew Word for Curse and Its Real Meaning," Messianic Revolution, accessed May 3, 2023, https://messianic-revolution.com/d27-16-the-hebrew-word-for-curse-and-its-real-meaning/.

Chapter 4

1. Online Etymology Dictionary, s.v. *"anathema,"* accessed May 3, 2023, https://www.etymonline.com/word/anathema.

Chapter 5

1. Alexander S. Gillis, "Algorithm," WhatIs.com, accessed May 3, 2023, https://www.techtarget.com/whatis/definition/algorithm.

2. "What Is Evolution?," YourGenome, accessed May 3, 2023, https://www.yourgenome.org/facts/what-is-evolution/.

3. Elizabeth Mixson, "What Is Quantum Computing?," AI Data & Analytics Network, January 18, 2022, https://www.aidataanalytics.network/data-science-ai/articles/what-is-quantum-computing.

4. Dictionary.com, s.v. "violation," accessed May 3, 2023, https://www.dictionary.com/browse/violation.

5. Bible Study Tools, s.v. *"pasha,"* accessed May 3, 2023, https://www.biblestudytools.com/lexicons/hebrew/kjv/pasha.html.

6. Alice G. Walton, "How Health and Lifestyle Choices Can Change Your Genetic Make-Up," *The Atlantic*, November 6, 2011, https://www.theatlantic.com/health/archive/2011/11/how-health-and-lifestyle-choices-can-change-your-genetic-make-up/247808/.

CHAPTER 6

1. "To Remember and Forget," Acts 242 Study, March 6, 2014, https://acts242study.com/to-remember-and-forget/.

2. Blue Letter Bible, s.v. *"azab,"* accessed May 3, 2023, https://www.blueletterbible.org/lexicon/h5800/rsv/wlc/0-1/.

3. Blue Letter Bible, s.v. *"azab."*

4. Blue Letter Bible, s.v. *"tāmē,"* accessed May 3, 2023, https://www.blueletterbible.org/lexicon/h2930/kjv/wlc/0-1/.

5. WordNet, "Contamination," Princeton University, accessed May 3, 2023, http://wordnetweb.princeton.edu/perl/webwn?s=contamination.

6. Dictionary.com, s.v. "unclean," accessed May 3, 2023, https://www.dictionary.com/browse/unclean.

7. Olusola Igbari, "Poverty and Corruption in the New Testament Perspective," *Open Access Library Journal* 3, no. 8 (August 2016): 1–8, doi: https://www.scirp.org/journal/paperinformation.aspx?paperid=70207.

8. Bible Study Tools, s.v. "sear" (*kausteriazo*), accessed May 3, 2023, https://www.biblestudytools.com/dictionary/sear/.

CHAPTER 7

1. Rev. David Wilson Rogers, "Do Not Bear False Witness," Carlsbad Current Argus, July 29, 2017, https://www.currentargus.com/story/life/faith/2017/07/29/do-not-bear-false-witness/517597001/.

2. Blue Letter Bible, s.v. "*ra,*" accessed May 3, 2023, https://www.blueletterbible.org/lexicon/h7451/kjv/wlc/0-1/.

3. Bible Study Tools, s.v. "wickedness," accessed May 3, 2023, https://www.biblestudytools.com/encyclopedias/isbe/wickedness.html.

4. *Merriam-Webster,* s.v. "profane," accessed May 3, 2023, https://www.merriam-webster.com/dictionary/profane.

5. Encyclopedia.com, s.v. "irrevocable," accessed May 3, 2023, https://www.encyclopedia.com/social-sciences-and-law/law/law/irrevocable.

CHAPTER 8

1. *All Hebrew Grammar in One Hour*, s.v. *"yahir,"* accessed Nay 3, 2023, https://www.pealim.com/dict/7528-yahir/.

2. Bible Hub, s.v. "glutton," accessed May 3, 2023, https://biblehub.com/topical/g/glutton.htm.

3. *Oxford English Dictionary*, s.v. "racism," accessed May 3, 2023, https://www.google.com/search?q=racism+definition.

4. Bible Hub, s.v. "dishonor," accessed May 3, 2023, https://biblehub.com/topical/d/dishonor.htm.

CHAPTER 9

1. *Oxford English Dictionary*, s.v. "pleading," accessed May 3, 2023, https://www.google.com/search?q=pleading+definition.

2. *Oxford English Dictionary*, s.v. "supplication," accessed May 3, 2023, https://www.google.com/search?q=supplication+definition.

3. *Oxford English Dictionary*, s.v. "petition," accessed May 3, 2023, https://www.google.com/search?q=petition+definition.

4. *Oxford English Dictionary*, s.v. "posture," accessed May 3, 2023, https://www.google.com/search?q=posture+definition.

5. *Oxford English Dictionary*, s.v. "persistence," accessed May 3, 2023, https://www.google.com/search?q=persistence+definition.

6. *Oxford English Dictionary*, s.v. "patience," accessed May 3, 2023, https://www.google.com/search?q=patience+definition.

7. *Oxford English Dictionary*, s.v. "pronouncement," accessed May 3, 2023, https://www.google.com/search?q=pronouncement+definition.

8. *Oxford English Dictionary*, s.v. "petition," accessed May 3, 2023, https://www.google.com/search?q=petition+definition.

9. "What Is a Petition? Definition, How It Works, and Example," Investopedia, March 5, 2022, https://www.investopedia.com/terms/p/petition.asp.

ABOUT THE AUTHOR

ALEXANDER PAGANI IS THE founder of Amazing Church in the Bronx, New York. He is an apostolic Bible teacher with keen insight into the realm of the demonic, generational curses, and deliverance. An internationally sought-after conference speaker, he takes an uncompromising approach to the Scriptures and has been involved in more than four hundred deliverance sessions. He has appeared on various television networks, including TBN and The Word Network. An honorary graduate of Central Pentecostal Bible Institute, he carries a spirit of wisdom and discernment to unlock secrets of the kingdom with signs and wonders following his ministry. Pagani is the best-selling author of *The Secrets to Deliverance* and was featured in the 2023 film *Come Out in Jesus Name*. He lives in New York with his wife, Ibelize, and their sons, Apollos and Xavier.